THE
FUNCTIONS
OF
PREJUDICE

UPTOWN is People Sticking TOGETHER

THE FUNCTIONS OF PREJUDICE

Jack Levin

Northeastern University

HARPER & ROW, PUBLISHERS
New York   Evanston   San Francisco   London

For my mother and father with love

To the memory of Richie Arches,
friend and student, whose
impact on society lives beyond
his untimely death.

Sponsoring Editor: Alvin A. Abbott
Project Editor: Pamela Landau
Designer: James McGuire
Production Supervisor: Stefania J. Taflinska
Picture Editor: Myra Schachne

The Functions of Prejudice

Library of Congress Cataloging in Publication Data
Levin, Jack, 1941–
    The functions of prejudice.
    Bibliography: p.
    1. Discrimination—United States.   2. Prejudices and antipathies.
    3. Minorities—-United States.
I. Title.
HN57.L48   301.45'1042   74–14493
ISBN 0–06–043988–2

Grateful acknowledgment is made for use of photographs
on the following pages:
Frontispiece: Paul Sequeira, Rapho Guillumette
    Page x: Virginia Hamilton
    Page 38: Charles Gatewood
    Page 64: Wide World
    Page 88: Wide World
    Page 102: Wide World

Cover photograph: Sam Falk, Monkmeyer

CONTENTS

PREFACE

Recent decades have witnessed a growing awareness of the problems experienced by the minority groups in our society. Since the civil rights decision of the Supreme Court in 1954, the mass media have focused their attention on intergroup conflict and its now familiar issues. American colleges and universities have offered their students an unprecedented variety of courses relating to majority-minority conflict: its sociological, psychological, political, and economic dimensions. What is more, a number of social scientists have sought to identify the disadvantages of minority membership and to explain how the disadvantages are perpetuated.

The Functions of Prejudice attempts to provide a concise and readable introduction to the study of anti-minority prejudice and discrimination. A glance at the Contents of the book will disclose that it represents the perspective of more than a single discipline or school of thought, encompassing theories of prejudice from sociology as well as psychology, from functionalism as well as the conflict point of view.

If this book has some overall message to communicate, it is that majority-minority relations cannot be understood apart from the consequences of prejudice and discrimination. It is therefore necessary to examine *any* of the groups and individuals in a society that gain from the maintenance of the status quo, whether they be persons of power for whom prejudice serves economic or political ends, working-class persons whose sense of self-worth finds protection in the presence of prejudice, or certain elements of minorities whose special advantages would quickly disappear under the impact of full equality of opportunity.

I am indebted to a number of individuals—my friends, students, colleagues, editors, and family members—who contributed in important ways to the development and completion of this book. I am grateful to Norval Glenn, whose review of this work provided both incentive as well as direction at critical times. A debt of gratitude is also due Bob Bohlke, Toni Emrich, Max Hess, Lewis Killian, Ken MacDonald, and Patrick McNamara, who critically reviewed parts of an earlier manuscript or a proposal and suggested a number of significant improvements for the final version of this work. Sections of the manuscript also benefited from the comments of Cheryl Gilkes, John Ost, Max Shulman, and Linda Weinrich. Several insightful recommendations for the book were obtained in conversations with Joan and Richie Arches, Marcia Garrett, Pat Golden, Nina and Herb Greenwald, Louisa Howe, Norman Kaplan, Lila Leibowitz, Bill Levin, Sr., Marie Augusta Neal, Bernard Phillips, Dick Robbins, Alex Rysman, Jim Spates, Richard Swedberg, and Gerald Taube. At Harper & Row, Luther Wilson encouraged the original idea for the project and Al Abbott skillfully moved it to publication.

My wife, Flea, has once again played an essential part at all stages of my work. This time, however, she has also shared the pain that inevitably befalls the social scientist who ventures outside of his "ivory tower" and attempts to come to grips with an important issue of his time.

J.L.

THE
FUNCTIONS
OF
PREJUDICE

chapter one

THE NATURE OF PREJUDICE

People in our society differ with respect to the opportunities they have for acquiring wealth, status, and power. An individual's opportunities for success may depend in part upon such factors as talent, luck, experience, skill, and training; but they also depend upon the groups with which he can be identified. Thus, when all other qualifications are equalized, women have fewer opportunities than men; homosexuals have fewer opportunities than heterosexuals; the aged have fewer opportunities than youth; and blacks have fewer opportunities than whites.

We will be concerned here with the experiences of *minorities,* groups whose members have been assigned a subordinate position in a society by virtue of their race, religion, or country of origin (Sagarin, 1971; Vander Zanden, 1972). To focus upon the reasons why such persons are kept in a subordinate position, it is essential that we also examine the experiences of the *majority,* that group whose members hold a superordinate position with respect to wealth, status, and power, based on their race, religion, or country of origin. In American society, any departure from white, Anglo-Saxon, Protestant characteristics represents some deviation from the majority group and movement toward a minority (Gordon, 1964).

Numerical strength may have little to do with the ability to exercise power or maintain prestige. The *size* of a group does not necessarily determine whether its members have majority or minority status. Large numbers of individuals have been suppressed by a few. Numerically small groups have at least occasionally held sway. To take a modern example, a relatively small population of South African whites presently dominates the economy and political structure of a much more sizable population of South African blacks. Despite their numerical disadvantage, white South Africans clearly constitute a majority group in terms of their possession of wealth, status, and power.

In reality, individuals may hold simultaneous membership in both a majority group as well as a minority group (Vander Zanden, 1972). For instance, American Jews belong to a majority group with respect to their race (being classed as, and usually accepted as, white), but to a minority group with respect to their religion; black Americans are members of a racial minority, though many also hold membership in the religious majority (Protestantism).

Holding dual majority-minority membership has implications for extending the limits of majority-minority relations beyond the actions of white Protestant Americans against such groups as blacks, Mexican-Americans, or American Indians. We might also focus, for instance, on black anti-Semitism or on anti-black sentiment among Catholics and Jews, while maintaining our stress on the distinction between majority and minority.

The distinction between majority and minority is best treated as representing extreme end points against which the reality of social relations can be plotted and compared. In point of fact, group differences in power and privilege often turn out to be matters of degree rather than kind. To illustrate: White Protestants may have more power than white Catholics or Jews;

white Catholics or Jews, in turn, may have more power than blacks; blacks, in turn, may have more power than Puerto Ricans or American Indians.

CONCEPTIONS OF PREJUDICE

Social scientists have long sought to better understand the nature of prejudice against minorities—its origins, maintenance, and consequences. Many have expressed their concern about the debilitating impact of prejudice on the life-chances of minority-group members and on such attendant factors as "confusion of self-identity, lowered self-esteem, perception of the world as a hostile place, and serious sex-role conflicts" (Pettigrew, 1964:25). Others have focused their attention instead upon what influence prejudice has on the quality of moral life for all Americans, majority and minority alike. Myrdal (1944) in *An American Dilemma* depicts American race relations as posing a major moral struggle for white America since there is a deeply rooted conflict between the democratic values of the "American creed" and the social, political, and economic inequities experienced by American minorities.

Social scientists have traditionally regarded prejudice as destructive to society and to the individual. Directly or indirectly prejudice causes innocent persons to suffer, commits society's resources to antidemocratic if not unproductive ends, and does irreparable harm to the personality of the prejudiced individual. In the American experience alone, prejudice has been linked to a civil war, urban decay, crime and delinquency, and international tension.

Benign Prejudice

Another conception of prejudice has recently been advanced. Despite compelling evidence to indicate the malignancy of prejudice, some social scientists imply that prejudice can no longer be held accountable for the poverty, miseducation, or underemployment presently experienced by members of certain minority groups in our society. Their argument usually runs as follows: Though initially responsible for the problems of minority groups (for example, "back in the days of slavery"), prejudice or racism of the majority is no longer to blame for such problems. Current prejudice is regarded as benign, secondary, or irrelevant to an understanding of minority problems. The minority group is viewed as trapped in a self-feeding vicious circle of deprivation that is difficult if not impossible to reverse. Ryan (1971) calls this view *blaming-the-victim*.

The most common form of blaming-the-victim has to do with the cultural deprivations to which a minority-group member is presumably exposed. As a case in point, Ryan considers a slum child who is blamed for his own miseducation. The focus here is on the alleged defects of the child: his lack of exposure to books and magazines, the absence of encouragement or support from his parents, and his own impulsiveness. By confining attention to the child and to deficiencies in his home environment, it is possible to overlook the ". . . collapsing buildings and torn textbooks, the frightened, insensitive teachers, the six additional desks in the room, the blustering, frightened principals, the relentless segregation, the callous administrator, the irrelevant curriculum, the bigoted or cowardly members of the school board, the insulting history book, the stingy taxpayers, the fairly-tale readers, or the self-serving faculty of the local teachers' college" (Ryan, 1971:4).

The benign prejudice viewpoint provides the basis for a convenient, if not convincing, rationalization for those who seek to justify the status quo with respect to majority-minority relations. As noted by Armendáriz, the experiences of Mexican-Americans may be all too characteristic:

1. The representative of a large corporation in Corpus Christi argued that the reason why only eight of his 883 employees are Mexican-Americans has nothing at all to do with

discrimination. He claims that he has not been able to locate qualified applicants.

2. A union official testified that the refusal of his trade council to accept applications for training under OEO programs from Mexican-American applicants does not constitute prejudice or discrimination. His union requires a high school education and a special examination in order to qualify as a house painter.

3. A corporation personnel executive insisted that his Mexican-American employees are unqualified for promotion, yet the white Americans who receive the desired positions are actually less qualified than their Mexican-American counterparts in terms of education as well as other criteria.

4. A school administrator argued that the charge of illegal segregation in Mexican-American schools is due to the concentration of Mexican-Americans in certain school districts. He knows, of course, that a simple alteration in district boundaries would produce integrated schools. [Armendáriz, 1967.]

In order to explain the persistence of socioeconomic inequalities between majority and minority groups, some social scientists have posited the existence of a *culture of poverty* (Lewis, 1968), a way of life that includes shared views about desirable and undesirable behavior as well as adaptational techniques and institutions for coping with the problems of a lower-class existence. But such a conception of a culture of poverty depicts more than just a way of adapting to a set of conditions imposed by the majority group:

> Once it comes into existence . . . [the culture of poverty]
> . . . tends to perpetuate itself from generation to generation
> because of its effect on the children. By the time slum
> children are age six or seven, they have usually absorbed
> the basic values and attitudes of their subculture and are not

psychologically geared to take full advantage of the changing conditions or increased opportunities that may occur in their lifetime. [Lewis, 1968:188.]

Whatever its intent or effect, the notion of a vicious circle of cultural deprivation to account for minority-group problems has gained widespread acceptance among social scientists and laymen alike. Moynihan gave it official recognition and acceptance when as Assistant Secretary of Labor he asserted: "At the heart of the deterioration of the fabric of Negro society is the deterioration of the Negro family. It is the fundamental source of the weakness of the Negro community at the present time" (1965:51).

Another version of benign prejudice has developed from the work of those who assume a genetic basis of group differences in intelligence. During the early part of this century, psychologists found that immigrants coming from Poland, Russia, Greece, Turkey, and Italy, tended to score lower on intelligence tests than immigrants coming from northwestern Europe. "Psychologists of the time did a host of studies to demonstrate that what they called Mediterranean-Latin-Slavic people, having done much worse on intelligence tests than 'Nordics,' had to be genetically stupid, and that if they were admitted to this country in large numbers they would lower the national level of intelligence" (Kamin, 1973:22). This finding and its interpretation became a basis for the restrictive immigration laws of the 1920s.

Addressing himself to the issue of group differences in intellectual capacity among immigrants to the United States, a Princeton University psychologist argued in 1923:

Immigration should not only be restrictive but highly selective. And the revision of the immigration and naturalization laws will only afford a slight relief from our present difficulty. The really important steps are those looking toward the prevention of the continued propagation of defective strains in the present population. If all immigration were stopped now, the decline of American intelligence would still be inevitable. This is the problem which must be met, and our manner of meeting it will determine the future course of our national life. [Brigham, 1923:210.]

In a like manner, Sweeny wrote in *North American Review* that the time had come to awaken to the need for protection from the influx of the "worthless" Eastern and Southern European immigrants who scored lower on intelligence tests than their counterparts from Western and Northern Europe. He argued that the "stream of intelligence" was being "polluted" by "this emptying of undesirables into this country . . ." (1922:600).

The argument that minority-group members are genetically inferior is by no means a new one, but there has recently been renewed interest in it in the United States. For many, the re-emergence of this view in social science is best represented by Arthur Jenson, an educational psychologist who revised the hypothesis that "genetic factors are strongly implicated in the average Negro-white intelligence difference" (1969:82). In a subsequent article, Richard Herrnstein (1971) similarly suggested that socioeconomic status may be based on inherited differences in intelligence, permitting the development of an "hereditary meritocracy" for American society in which intellectually superior individuals will rule.* Whether based on en-

* The benign prejudice viewpoint also finds expression in explanations of social role and intellectual differences between men and women based on physiological models. As recently noted by Liebowitz, ". . . these academic investigations into sex differences come at the same time as revivals of notions of innate differences in intellectual capacities between blacks and whites. Both revivals, it would seem, are a response to active efforts at implementing liberal, non-biogenetic social role analyses which gained respectability during and after World War II" (1973:1).

SURGERY FOR SOCIAL VIOLENCE: A CASE OF "BENIGN PREJUDICE"

Soon after the Detroit riots in 1967, an important letter appeared in the *Journal of the American Medical Association*. The authors acknowledged that the social causes of urban rioting are "well known," and that the "urgent needs" of the underprivileged should not be minimized. But they did not propose to deal with these causes or needs. They focused instead on the search for, "the more subtle role of other possible factors, including brain dysfunction in the rioters who engaged in arson, sniping and physical assault."

. . . the authors of this letter warned that we shouldn't believe the urgent social and economic needs of the ghetto are solely responsible for urban riots. "If slum conditions alone determined and initiated riots," they asked, "why are the vast majority of slum-dwellers able to resist the temptations of unrestrained violence? Is there something peculiar about the violent slum-dweller that differentiates him from his peaceful neighbor?

After raising these "scientific" questions, the authors proceeded to cite evidence showing that focal lesions in the brain are capable of spurring "senseless" violent outbursts. Although the available evidence comes from patients with long-standing histories of severe epilepsy, they concluded that violent behavior in general likely has a comparable biological basis. They insisted that, "we need intensive research and clinical studies of the *individuals* committing the violence. The goal of such studies would be to pinpoint, diagnose and treat those people with low violence thresholds before they contribute to further tragedies."

SOURCE: Excerpted from *Psychology Today* Magazine, October, 1973. Copyright © Ziff Davis Publishing Company.

vironmental or hereditary premises, such arguments contribute to an acceptance of the view that the subordinate status of American minorities is not attributable in large part to the prejudices of the majority. This represents an acceptable viewpoint for members of our society who have an investment in the status quo or who experience the burden of guilt for their attitudes or behavior regarding minorities.

The Functions of Prejudice

Conceptions of prejudice influence our thinking about the nature of majority-minority relations. Benign prejudice alerts us to the possibility of a vicious circle of deprivation and to the presence of special adaptational techniques in the subculture of poverty. Despite the good intentions of its spokesmen, however, this approach, which emphasizes characteristics of the "victim," has with too few exceptions tended to ignore the fact—as pointed out by the U.S. Advisory Commission on Civil Disorders in 1968—that "white society is deeply implicated in the ghetto. White institutions created it, white institutions maintain it, and white society condones it" (p. 2).

By contrast, those social scientists who emphasize the harmful impact of prejudice on the members of our society—focusing, for example, on the mistreatment of blacks, Puerto Ricans, Mexican-Americans, and Jews—have served to reduce misconceptions and stereotypes about such minorities and to clarify some basic issues surrounding the state of intergroup relations in the United States. Most importantly, the traditional approach has provided a well-documented justification for laws, social movements, and individual efforts that seek to reduce the level of prejudice in our society. Unfortunately, by emphasizing the harmful and costly impact of prejudice, this approach may also have obscured an essential characteristic of prejudice—a characteristic that may help to explain its tenacious hold on our society and its ability to thrive and prosper across many generations of Americans. What has been too little recognized previously is that prejudice performs some important positive functions for certain groups in our society.*

* Some social scientists have recognized the need to explore the positive functions of prejudice or racism. See, for example, Bettelheim

Following Merton's (1957) usage, we shall define *function* as a consequence that aids in the adaptation or adjustment of a system. In the case of a *manifest function*, such a consequence may be intentional and recognized by the members of a system; in regard to a *latent function,* however, a consequence may be neither intentional nor recognized by system participants. For example, the manifest function of a marriage ceremony is to legally unite the bride and groom, while a latent function may be to increase family solidarity by providing an occasion for family members to come together in a common activity. As another example, the manifest function of television may be entertainment; one of its latent functions is the socialization of the audience to middle-class norms and values.

Also in accordance with Merton's functionalism, we shall recognize a range of levels—personality, culture, subgroup, society—for which any given item may have consequences. A particular item may aid in the adaptation of personality but not society, or an item may be beneficial to one subgroup but costly in some way to another.

It is a major thesis of this work that prejudice persists in our society precisely because it continues to have adaptive benefits—latent and manifest, long term and short term, psychological and sociological—for elements of the majority group as well as the minority group. It follows that we then can only reduce prejudice and attendant majority-minority inequities to the extent that we actually come to grips with the important functions that prejudice serves.

Our usage of the term *function* should be sharply distinguished from a value judgment regarding the "goodness" of a phenomenon. An ardent women's liberationist might very well investigate the ego-defensive functions of sexism for the

---

and Janowitz (1965), Blauner (1972), Chinoy (1961), Dollard (1937), Glenn (1965), Heer (1959), McWilliams (1948), Metzger (1971), Rose (1974), Simpson and Yinger (1972), Tumin (1965), and Vander Zanden (1972).

maintenance of the male chauvinist's personality—her primary goal being to better understand how sexism operates and how it can be reduced. A political analyst might examine the latent social functions of the political machine among immigrants for the purpose of proposing viable functional alternatives. A student of international affairs might study the adaptive uses of nationalism in order to gain insight into strategies for breaking down barriers between peoples. A criminologist might conduct research into the positive functions of murder in order to discover why it occurs so frequently.

Whether or not prejudice can be regarded as good may be independent of the conclusions reached in a functional analysis. In the first place, prejudice can be viewed by an individual or by society as a whole as an immoral act, and therefore an unacceptable means, regardless of its relative costs and benefits, for the maintenance of a given system. Societies have made such judgments regarding the functional phenomena of adultery, murder, rape, cannibalism, and prostitution, to mention only a few. Secondly, the functions of prejudice do not influence all members of society or its subgroups to the same extent, but operate quite selectively within a narrow range. For instance, prejudice may turn out to be politically functional only for the extremely powerful elements of a majority group; prejudice may be severely injurious to a minority group as a whole, but have adaptive utility for certain subgroups within it; or, prejudice may be costly for society in general though having positive consequences for its affluent members. Finally, functional analysis addresses itself to the adaptive mechanisms of any system or group. Therefore, the system or group itself need not be held in esteem by those who decide to study it. For instance, a Black Muslim might conduct a functional analysis of the Ku Klux Klan just as a member of the Jewish Defense League might study the functions of anti-Semitism in Russia. As Tumin suggests, "Nothing need be said about the desirability or undesirability of the system; indeed, nothing *may* be said if functionalism, so conceived, is to be scientifically neutral" (1965:380).

In line with the foregoing conception of prejudice, the two-fold purpose of the present work is to (1) identify and analyze the range of important personality and social functions that prejudice performs, especially in the context of American society, and (2) focus on certain characteristics of American society that help to explain why prejudice continues to be functional for certain groups. Before these objectives can be realized, however, we must first examine the nature of prejudice.

A DEFINITION OF PREJUDICE

In its original usage, the word *prejudice* referred to a "pre-judgment," or an evaluation or decision made before the facts of a case could be properly determined and weighed. This usage was subsequently broadened to include "any unreasonable attitude that is unusually resistant to rational influence" (Rosnow, 1972:53). Thus, an individual who stubbornly committed himself to a position in the face of overwhelming evidence to the contrary could be characterized as prejudiced, whether about his children, his politics, his religious convictions, or his friends. Such a broad concept of prejudice may be useful in everyday conversation since it draws our attention to the unfortunate tendency for individuals to jump to conclusions and to make dogmatic judgments, but for purposes of the present work, we must assign a more limited meaning.

So that prejudice can be examined within a single, over-arching, theoretical framework, we begin by defining it as *interpersonal hostility which is directed against individuals based on their membership in a minority group.* Using this definition of prejudice, we can from the outset exclude the following kinds of phenomena from the purview of our analysis:

1. prejudices *not* directed against human beings (e.g., pre-judgments about animals, cars, and houses);

2. preferences in interpersonal relations *not* based on group membership (e.g., a situation in which two individuals can't get along because each tries to dominate the relationship).

Our concept of prejudice is meant to focus our attention throughout this analysis squarely on *negative* feelings, beliefs, and action-tendencies, or discriminatory acts, that arise *against human beings* by virtue of the status they occupy or are perceived to occupy as members of a minority group. It is in this restricted sense that prejudice, whether against blacks, Puerto Ricans, Mexican-Americans, or American Indians, has come to be regarded by social scientists as a troublesome and costly phenomenon, not only for the target of prejudice but for the prejudiced individual and the larger society as well.

PREJUDICE AS ATTITUDE

The nature of prejudice can be examined in part at the level of individual attitudes. Individuals hold favorable and unfavorable attitudes that help to orient them toward the myriad persons, objects, and concepts in their lives, such as their parents, friends, nation, and religion. From a psychological perspective, prejudice can be regarded as *a negative attitude toward the members of a minority group* (Ehrlich, 1972; Kramer, 1949). As such, prejudice is a learned disposition consisting of the following components or dimensions:

1. negative beliefs or stereotypes

2. negative feelings or emotions

3. the tendency to discriminate

Negative Stereotypes

In the words of Walter Lippman (1922), *stereotypes* are "pictures in our heads," beliefs that we hold regarding the members of a category. In the present context, we are specifically concerned with beliefs or stereotypes that have become associated with various categories of minority groups. Oftentimes, such stereotypes are overgeneralized to an extent that no members of the minority can avoid inclusion: *all* Blacks are lazy, *all* Mexican-Americans are treacherous, *all* Jews are mercenary, *all* Puerto Ricans are dirty, *all* Chinese are sly, *all* Turks are cruel. Frequently, however, the prejudiced individual may have to treat contrary evidence—instances that don't fit his stereotype—as exceptions to the rule. Bettelheim and Janowitz report the following beliefs about Jewish soldiers as expressed by an especially prejudiced veteran of World War II:

> They shirk their duty, they're no combat men. Some will fight, I'll give them that credit, but most of them are out for themselves. If he has a chance to save himself, he'll save himself. A Jew will never give you nothing for nothing either. (But) I've found a couple of good Jews, like in any nationality, but only a few. [1964:139.]

Traits admired or revered in the members of an ingroup may be regarded as deplorable when ascribed to outgroup members. As Allport observed, Abraham Lincoln was seen as "thrifty, hard-working, eager for knowledge, ambitious, devoted to the rights of the average man, and eminently successful in climbing the ladder of opportunity," whereas Jews are viewed as "tight-fisted, over-ambitious, pushing, and radical" (1954:189). In a similar way, anti-Semitic veterans describe effective combat behavior as "courageous" if carried out by non-Jewish soldiers, but "bloodthirsty" if the same behavior is carried out by Jewish soldiers (Bettelheim and Janowitz, 1964:139).

Stereotyping frequently contains an element of *projection,* whereby negative characteristics of the prejudiced individual become associated with the members of a minority. For example, Anglo-Americans have been known to project onto Mexican-Americans the very attributes which they themselves had exemplified in the conquest of Mexicans and their land. Mexicans were regarded as natural-born thieves who indiscriminately stole livestock from white settlers, yet white cattle barons were noted for stealing livestock from powerless border Mexicans. Mexicans were also widely regarded as treacherous and cruel (attributable in part to their "Indian blood"), yet the Texas Rangers, lynch mobs, the U.S. army, white sheriffs, and drunken cowhands often murdered innocent Mexicans without fear of punishment (Jacobs and Landau, 1971).

What are the stereotypes about minority groups that have traditionally been held by the members of American society? In a pioneering study of ethnic stereotypes, Katz and Braly (1933) sought to provide a partial answer by investigating the characteristics ascribed by one hundred Princeton undergraduates to various racial and ethnic groups. Their findings indicated a high level—sometimes reaching 75 percent—of agreement among the Princeton students that

> Jews are "shrewd," "mercenary," and "industrious"
> Blacks are "superstitious," "lazy," and "happy-go-lucky"
> Turks are "cruel," "very religious," and "treacherous"
> Chinese are "superstitious," "sly," and "conservative"
> Italians are "artistic," "impulsive," and "passionate"
> Irish are "pugnacious," "quick tempered," and "witty."

Bettelheim and Janowitz, in their study of one hundred and fifty World War II veterans, similarly found much consensus that Jews "have the money," "run the country," "use under-

MASS MEDIA ADVERTISEMENTS THAT PORTRAY ANTI-MEXICAN STEREOTYPES

Advertiser	Content of Ad	The Message
Granny Goose	Fat Mexican has guns, ammunition	Mexicans are overweight and carry weapons
Frito-Lay	"Frito-Bandito"	Mexicans are sneaky thieves
Liggett & Meyers	"Paco" never "feen-ishes" anything, not even revolution	Mexicans are too lazy to improve themselves
A.J. Reynolds	Mexican bandit	Mexicans are thieves
Camel Cigarettes	"Typical" Mexican village, all asleep or bored	Mexicans are do-nothings and irre-sponsible people
General Motors	White man holds Mexicans at gunpoint	Mexicans should be arrested by superior white men
Lark	Mexican house painter is covered with paint	Mexicans are sloppy workers
Philco-Ford	Mexican is sleeping by a TV set	Mexicans are always sleeping
Frigidaire	Mexican banditos are interested in a freezer	Mexicans are thieves who want Anglo artifacts
Arrid	While Mexican sprays underarm, voice says, "If it works for him, it will work for you."	Mexicans stink more

SOURCE: Adapted from Thomas M. Martínez 1969 "Advertising and Racism: The Case of the Mexican-American." El Grito (Summer): 27.

handed business methods," and are "clannish," while blacks "depreciate property," are "dirty," and "lazy" (1964:141–142).

Widely shared stereotypes about America's ethnic groups have found their way into the mass communication messages of our society. As early as 1946, Berelson and Salter analyzed the characters in popular magazine fiction to find stereotypical portrayals for virtually every minority and foreign group in their fictional population. The following are only a few examples of the stereotyped treatment found in this sample of stories:

The Italian Gangster.   Louie di Paolo, an amiable racketeer with a debt of loyalty to an heiress, furnishes her with money and a kidnapping so that she can get her own way with a young man. Louie is "a sinister-looking individual with a white scar over one eye . . . known as Blackie, Two Rod, and Smart 'Em Up in various police precincts, and among the underworld citizenry. . . ." Says he: " 'Beer was my racket. I made my pile and been layin' low ever since: If you want twenty-five G's, all I got to do is stick up my own safe-deposit box.' " He drives "a coupe with bulletproof glass and a specially built steel body, ready for anything."

The Sly and Shrewd Jew.   Jew Jake, manager of a troop of barnstorming stunt flyers, shows greater concern for money than for the safety of his employees. He has an "ungainly and corpulent figure" and he rubs his hands "in a familiar and excited gesture." In answer to his question, " 'Maybe you'd like to make five bucks easy?' " the hero says: " 'Jake, you would not put out five bucks for anything less than a suicide.' " Another character says: " 'You ought to know the way Jake is. He'd like it better if I did not pull it (the parachute cord) at all. It would give the customers a thrill.' "

The Emotional Irish.   Ellen, an Irish cook, is overwhelmed by her first sight of the new baby: "Ellen—who, being a Celt, was easily moved—flew out of the kitchen, saw a fraction of David's face, and burst into a flood of tears."

The Primitive and "Backward" Pole.   A Polish-American
girl thinks of escape from her national community. "I began
to despise our way of life. . . . The American men did
not value a wife who could work all day on her knees at his
side, taking only a day or two off to bear a child. They love
the weakness, not the strength in their women; love the job
of looking after and supporting them." [1946:180.]

Likewise, stereotyped descriptions of minority Americans
have been found in television programs (Smythe, 1954), magazine pictures (Shuey, 1953), textbooks (Cole and Wiese,
1954), motion pictures (McManus and Kronenberger, 1946),
newspapers (Simpson and Yinger, 1972), and comic strips
(Spiegelman, Terwilliger, and Fearing, 1953).

Negative Feelings

In his analysis of race relations in the United States, James
Comer, recounts the story of a white adolescent girl who was
scolded by her father for having put a coin in her mouth. "He
yelled, 'Get that money out of your mouth—it might have been
in a nigger's hand!' His message: blacks are untouchables, con-
taminating and not to be taken in or inserted" (1972:135).
Comer's story illustrates that stereotypes regarding a minority
group may be accompanied by negative *feelings* or emotions—
hatred, fear, revulsion, contempt, or envy—evoked by the
symbolic or actual presence of outgroup members:

The idea of patronizing a washroom, of eating at the same
restaurant, or of shaking hands with a Jew or black may
excite horror or disgust within some individuals. Black movement into a previously all-white neighborhood may produce
fear and anxiety among many whites. The social standing of
a prominent Jewish businessman or doctor may elicit envy
among some Gentiles. [Vander Zanden, 1972:21.]

When prejudice involves the emotional and the irrational, then it may become a more or less persistent characteristic of an individual, one that is deeply imbedded in his personality. In order to emphasize the enduring nature of prejudice, a social psychologist recently found the occasion to recall his early childhood experience in a poultry shop in a Jewish section of East Baltimore:

> How well I remember the dark little figure in the back room, the dread *shochet*, the ritual butcher; bent over his cutting board he resembled a brooding nursemaid at the bedside of her charge—except that he had a sinister blade in his right hand, and with his left hand was pinning a chicken to the board by the base of its throat, holding it steady for the one swift, effortless stroke. In an instant it was done. Blood spurted from the neck, the decapitated torso throbbed and trembled, the wings flapped wildly. And as the spasms subsided, a wave of nausea swept over me. To this day, I am unable to eat chicken. I find its flavor unpleasant, its odor worse, and its claim on the status of delicacy rather tenuous. [Rosnow, 1972:53.]

Negative feelings associated with minority groups may develop early in life and persist into adulthood, long after an individual has rid himself of prejudicial stereotypes or beliefs. In the words of Sartre (1965), an individual's prejudice may become his "passion." We will have more to say about the development of prejudice in children when we later view prejudice from a sociological perspective.

Tendency to Discriminate

Besides elements of belief and feeling, prejudice may also involve *action-tendency*, a disposition on the part of the prejudiced individual to *discriminate* against members of a given minority group. Recorded history is replete with examples of discrimination—instances of actual behavior ranging from the petty indignities of everyday interaction to acts of physical violence and slavery, many of which were perpetrated on a massive scale over the course of centuries.

In American society, the tendency to discriminate has often been translated into patterns of "social distance" whereby outgroup members are excluded from having personal relations with members of the dominant group. Since Bogardus developed his Social Distance Scale in 1925, numerous investigators have asked such groups as native white businessmen, school teachers, Jews, blacks, and white female college students to which level of the following scale they were willing to admit the members of various ethnic groups:

1. to close kinship by marriage
2. to my club as personal chums
3. to my street as neighbors
4. to employment in my occupation
5. to citizenship in my country
6. as visitors only to my country
7. would exclude from my country

Studies of social distance have yielded astonishingly consistent findings across groups: an unwillingness among Americans of diverse ethnic backgrounds and socioeconomic positions to have close social relations with blacks, Japanese, Chinese, Hindus, and Turks, and a widespread preference for individuals of English, German, and Spanish descent (Derbyshire and Brody, 1964).

Compare the social distance preferences that Bogardus obtained from samples of white businessmen and teachers, black Americans, and Jews (Simpson and Yinger, 1972:145):

110 *Native White* *Businessmen and* *School teachers*	*202* *Black* *Americans*	*178* *Native-Born* *Jews*
1. English	1. Negro	1. Jewish
2. French	2. French	2. English
3. German	3. Spanish	3. French
4. Spanish	4. English	4. German
5. Italian	5. Mexican	5. Spanish
6. Jewish	6. Hindu	6. Italian
7. Greek	7. Japanese	7. Mexican
8. Mexican	8. German	8. Japanese
9. Chinese	9. Italian	9. Turkish
10. Japanese	10. Chinese	10. Greek
11. Negro	11. Jewish	11. Chinese
12. Hindu	12. Greek	12. Hindu
13. Turkish	13. Turkish	13. Negro

Strong patterns of social distance have been uncovered by students of mass communication, reflecting the same tendencies to discriminate. For instance, Berelson and Salter's (1946) study of popular short stories revealed that "American" characters—white Protestants with no distinguishable ancestry of foreign origin—were rarely depicted as loving and marrying minority and foreign characters. Where marriage and love occurred in fiction, it was typically the American boy who courted and married the American girl. In a recent related study, Barcus and Levin (1966) similarly reported finding more intimate social relations between fictional characters of like ethnic background than between characters differing in this respect. Moreover, the preference for intragroup relations was found in both black as well as white magazine fiction.

The action-tendency dimension of prejudice (and, therefore, discrimination) often depends for support on the presence of derogatory stereotypes and feelings about the members of a minority group. Consider, for example, the well-entrenched system of discriminatory practices traditionally leveled against Mexican-Americans—a system of discrimination that has left a sizable economic and educational gap between Mexican-Americans and most other groups in our society (see Ten-Houten, Lei, Kendall, and Gordon, 1971). Stereotypes characterizing Mexican-Americans as being "unclean," "drunkards," "criminals," "deceitful," "unpredictable," and "immoral" serve to justify discrimination and exclusion in the following way: "If Mexicans are deceitful and immoral, they do not have to be accorded equal status and justice; if they are mysterious and unpredictable, there is no point in treating them as one would a fellow Anglo-American; and if they are hostile and dangerous, it is best that they live apart in colonies of their own" (Simmons, 1961:292).

Prejudicial beliefs and emotions sometimes become so intense that, in the eyes of majority members, members of a minority are totally separated, symbolically as well as physically, from the rest of humanity. Thus, when Sister Marie Augusta Neal recently visited South Africa on behalf of the Catholic Education Council, she found that some white South Africans refused to employ the term "people" in making reference to South African blacks.

PREJUDICE AS AN ELEMENT OF CULTURE

As we have seen, prejudiced attitudes may be widely shared among the members of a society. Americans separated by virtue of differences in region, ethnicity, or socioeconomic status nevertheless express surprisingly similar beliefs, feelings, and action-tendencies regarding the members of minority groups, especially blacks and Jews. What is more, prejudice often becomes an enduring characteristic of a society, being transmitted by its members from generation to generation, and re-

The three components of prejudice—negative beliefs, feelings, and action-tendencies—are generally consistent and mutually supportive. An individual who tends to accord differential treatment to blacks is likely to harbor negative feelings and stereotypes about them. It is also true, however, that inconsistencies frequently occur. For example, Merton's (1957) "fair-weather liberal" can be regarded as someone who may not have negative feelings or beliefs about the members of a minority; yet is ready to discriminate against them in order to gain social approval or financial reward. This type is illustrated by restaurant owners in border states who denied having negative feelings about blacks but refused to serve them for fear they would lose customers. Another possibility is the "timid bigot," an individual who harbors negative feelings or beliefs about the members of a minority but who is not predisposed to take action against them. "If the situation—as defined by law or custom—precludes open discrimination, he conforms: he serves Negro customers, sits next to them on buses or trains, sends his children to school with Negro children. 'What can I do,' he says, 'fight the system, fight city hall?' " [Rose, 1974:105.]

ceiving strong support in the form of custom or the enforcement of legal codes. To take an extreme example, Indian students continue to carry caste stereotypes similar to those which have existed for many generations despite radical changes in India's traditional caste relations (Sinha and Sinha, 1967).

Far from being deviant or abnormal, prejudice often becomes the normal and expected state of affairs in a society. From a sociological point of view, therefore, we can regard prejudice *as an element of the culture—the normative order— of the society in which it exists* (Westie, 1964).

When prejudice is cultural, we learn it through socialization just as we learn other conceptions of "what ought to be"— conceptions such as motherhood, patriotism, love of church, and economic achievement. Prejudice transmitted by agents of socialization including parents, peers, and teachers represents

As a cultural phenomenon, prejudice frequently finds widespread approval. The writer of the following passages—an Islander of part-Hawaiian ancestry—illustrates that the acceptance by members of a minority of the prejudice directed against them can lead to severe forms of self-hatred:

> I think I waste a lot of my time on my own kind, I mean the Hawaiians. They are not enlightened, not developing, not progressive people. . . . All they do is to eat and sleep and play the guitar.

> I'm a Hawaiian myself and I hate to say this, but I don't care much for them . . . they are not ambitious people. Their only ambition is to play music. They don't care for anything else. Then you see a Hawaiian does not come to work after a pay-day. Pay-day today and the next day no work. I don't know what they do with their money, but I think they drink a lot. . . .

> .   .   .

> They are so dirty. They eat just like pigs with their hands. Gee, there's one Hawaiian boy who sits right next to me . . . and his feet are full of dirt and mud. Gee! dirty, can't stand it! And over here (pointing to his neck) full of dirt. When I see him like that, I turn my back to him.

> I hate Hawaiians, oh, I hate Hawaiians! If you treat 'em good they come back and treat you bad. If you do good to them, they do bad to you. They talk about you and tell all kinds of things about you. That's true, I feel this way. If you say something they tell people something you never said. That's how they make trouble. . . .

> I hate Hawaiian! Oh, Hawaiian kind of low. I wish I didn't have any Hawaiian blood. I regret I have Hawaiian blood.

SOURCE: Margaret M. Lam 1936 "Racial Myth and Family Tradition-Worship Among Part-Hawaiians." *Social Forces* (March):156.

an expression of firmly established and widely held ideals regarding the character of social relationships. Thus, the acceptance of prejudice may begin early in life. Comer relates the story of the wife of a black physician in Mississippi who was followed down the street by a two-year-old white toddler dressed only in a diaper who pointed at her yelling "nigger, nigger" (1972:135).

By age three, most children seem to be aware of ethnic differences. Moreover, there seems to be a strong preference for "whiteness" on the part of both black and white preschool children. For example, when asked to choose between a white and a brown doll identical in every other respect, *black and white* preschoolers express strong preferences for the white doll, which they perceive as being "the doll they want to play with best," "the doll that is good," and "the doll that is a nice color." By contrast, the brown doll tends to be viewed as "the doll they don't want to play with," "the doll that is bad," and "the doll that is not a nice color" (Clark and Clark, 1947; Greenwald and Oppenheim, 1968; Morland, 1958). As shown by Morland (1969), these findings cannot be a result of a universal preference for "whiteness," since Chinese children in Hong Kong prefer and identify with dolls representing their own race rather than Caucasians.

Prejudicial Norms in American Society

As an element of culture, prejudice against certain minorities has throughout the history of American society been translated into *ideal norms* regarding the proper behavior of minorities in their dealings with members of the dominant group. From the 1600s, rules governing the enslavement of black Americans permitted separating the children of slaves from their parents and forbade legal marriages between slaves. In the antebellum South, black Americans could not own books, inherit money, learn to read or write, or vote. Even in nonslavery states before

1865, anti-black norms were imposed and rigorously enforced by whites. Northern blacks could not vote, enter hotels or restaurants (except in the role of servants), and were segregated from whites with respect to formal education, trains, steamboats, church-seating, and theaters (Burkey, 1971).

Anti-black norms thrived for more than a century following the Civil War, despite the abolition of slavery and the establishment of a short period of Reconstruction. In most regions of the United States, blacks were restricted to entering the most undesirable occupations and continued to be segregated from whites in terms of formal education, membership in unions, public accommodations, and housing. Moreover, especially in the South, blacks were subjected to a complex system of petty indignities. Such restrictions included prohibitions against interracial dating, against social visits by blacks to the homes of whites, against sexual relations between black men and white women, and even against blacks interrupting conversations between whites. Intergroup norms required, for example, that physicians serve their white patients before their black patients, that blacks remove their hats when in the presence of whites, that black domestics enter the homes of whites by the back door, and that black automobile drivers yield the right-of-way to their white counterparts (Burkey, 1971).

Playing the Role

Negative stereotypes and feelings about a minority group that become widely shared and enduring elements of a culture often assume the force of prescribed *roles* which outgroup members are expected to play. The complex network of formal and informal norms regarding the relationship between black and white Americans generated what Pettigrew (1964) has called the social role of "Negro," a label prescribing that black Americans "play the game" by "wearing their masks" and acting out the role of the inferior in dealings with whites. Under the American form of slavery, for example, blacks were expected to be unconditionally obedient to their masters and to express respect for all whites (Blassingame, 1972). Slaves often "played the role assigned to them, acted the clown, and curried the favor of their masters in order to win the maximum rewards within the system" (Silberman, 1964:79).

Many of the stereotypes traditionally associated with black Americans actually became their role prescriptions. Blacks were supposed to be "lazy" and "happy-go-lucky." If they should have refused to play this role, blacks were usually evaluated by whites as "not knowing their place" and, as a result, were ridiculed, discouraged, ignored, or severely punished (Redding, 1950). So goes the Herblock cartoon, "You don't understand boy. You're supposed to just shuffle along." Those who removed their masks and dared to not shuffle risked the consequences of their actions. Yet those who played the role of "Negro" also paid dearly, as illustrated in the work of Paul Laurence Dunbar, a black poet who lived at the turn of this century. He wrote,

> We smile, but O great Christ, our cries
> To thee from tortured souls arise.
> We sing, but oh, the clay is vile
> Beneath our feet, and long the mile;
> But let the world dream otherwise,
> We wear the mask. [1940:14.]

We emphasize the distinction between expected and prescribed role, for it may help to explain why the nature of discrimination has differed depending upon the minority group against whom it was directed. As we have seen, many stereotypes about black Americans have represented both expected as well as prescribed behavior (for example, blacks are *expected* to be and *ought* to be "lazy" and "happy-go-lucky"). If they played the game and fulfilled their stereotype, blacks were usually permitted by the dominant group to survive and perpetuate themselves as a group, though being robbed of their dignity and self-esteem. By contrast, many stereotypes about Jews have involved expected but *proscribed* behavior (for example, Jews are *expected* to but *ought not* to "have the money," "run the country," and be "shrewd"). As a result, though Jews could maintain their cultural heritage, many Jews were not permitted to remain within a society, especially if they played the game and fulfilled their stereotypes.

THE PERSISTENCE OF PREJUDICE

American society has recently experienced a downward trend in regard to prejudiced attitudes against such minorities as blacks and Jews. Traditional stereotypes, negative feelings, and discriminatory practices apparently have to some degree eroded with the passage of time and, more importantly, with the passage of appropriate legislation as well as activism on the part of minorities. There is some evidence that younger generations of Americans may indeed be demonstrating greater tolerance and more careful thinking about ethnic groups than did their older counterparts in former generations (Karlings, Coffman, and Walters, 1969). As determined by large-scale surveys of white racial attitudes from 1942 to 1968, for example, there was a sizeable increase in the proportion of white Northerners as well as Southerners willing to support the integration of the schools. Over the same period of time, the proportion of white Americans who regarded the intelligence of blacks as equal to that of whites rose considerably in both the North and the South (Bellisfield, 1972–1973; Hyman and Sheatsley, 1956 and 1964). Data from a series of surveys of the American population in 1964, 1968, and 1970 suggest that white and black attitudes have not moved farther apart on questions regarding principle and policy, but, in fact, may have moved somewhat closer together (Campbell, 1970).

Despite a decline in the overall level of prejudice, however, the evidence is all too compelling that prejudice still has a tenacious hold on many members of American society, persisting at an alarming level especially against such groups as blacks, Puerto Ricans, Mexican-Americans, American Indians, and Jews, and showing few signs of further abatement. In a recent study, Karlins, Coffman, and Walters (1969) compared the stereotypes held by Princeton undergraduates in 1967 with those found in the earlier study by Katz and Braly (1933) and in a 1951 replication by Gilbert. The findings of Karlins, Coffman, and Walters failed to support the contention that minority stereotypes have necessarily been fading. Instead, traditional stereotypes that may have declined in their frequency of usage seemed to be replaced by other stereotypes, in many cases resembling the original ones. For example, the old view of blacks as being "superstitious" and "lazy" gave way to the view that they were "musical," "happy-go-lucky," "lazy," and "ostentatious." In a similar way, rather than being stereotyped as "pugnacious" as in previous studies, the Irish were seen as primarily "quick tempered" and "extremely nationalistic."

The substitution of traditional stereotypes for new ones may have become incorporated into the mass media images of minority groups. For example, a 1953 study by Shuey of popular magazine advertisements concluded that blacks were being stereotypically portrayed as servants, porters, and waiters. A similar analysis of magazine advertisements appearing between 1965 and 1970 determined that advertising still perpetuated racial stereotypes, though in more subtle ways:

> Indeed, if the advertising image were to be believed, the black is a record star, an entertainer, a celebrity; if not one of these, he is a child, a woman, or a foreigner. As a male, he is in need of public or private charity, and he seldom if ever enjoys the occupational status of the whites with whom he is depicted. Missing from these ads are black families and black

males, at work and at leisure—in short, the black American,
rather than the black stereotype. [Colfax and Sternberg,
1972:17.]

Though changes have occurred, there is reason to believe
that many of our long-standing traditional stereotypes have
been maintained intact. Selznick and Steinberg (1969), in their
interviews with a representative cross section of the national
population in 1964, found that 54 percent of their respondents
thought "Jews always like to be at the head of things," 52 percent agreed that "Jews stick together too much," and 42 percent
felt that "Jews are more willing than others to use shady
practices to get what they want" (p. 6). Moreover, Petroni
(1972) found frequent usage of minority group stereotypes
among white, midwestern, high school students, who were
highly critical of the prejudices of their parents and yet who
failed to recognize they had prejudices of their own.

With reference to stereotypes associated with blacks, Brink
and Harris (1964) reported that a substantial proportion of a
nationwide cross section of white Americans taken in 1963—
in some cases reaching almost 70 percent agreement—were
willing to agree that blacks

laugh alot
tend to have less ambition
smell different
have looser morals
keep untidy homes
want to live off the handout
have less native intelligence
breed crime
are inferior to whites
care less for the family.

In a 1966 survey, Brink and Harris (1967) again conducted a
nationwide study of white Americans, finding a softening in

some of their negativism regarding blacks, but still reporting about 50 percent who agreed that blacks "laugh alot," "smell different," "have looser morals," and "want to live off the handout." Campbell's 1968 survey determined that of the whites living in the fifteen cities studied,

> 67% say Negroes are pushing too fast for what they want,

> 56% believe that Negro disadvantages in jobs, education, and housing are due mainly to Negroes themselves rather than to discrimination,

> 51% oppose laws to prevent racial discrimination in housing,

> 33% say that if they had small children they would rather they have only white friends, and

> 24% of those old enough to vote say they would not vote for a qualified Negro of their own party preference who was running for mayor. [Campbell, 1970:4–5.]

Thus, the findings of recent surveys of American attitudes strongly suggest that hostile stereotypes and feelings regarding various minorities are being perpetuated in American life. Moreover, white Americans continue to resist the possible integration of significant numbers of blacks (Knapp and Alston, 1972–1973). Reflecting on the data from a 1968 national survey of American adults, Levy (1972) reports a "polarization in racial attitudes" and concludes that "the prognosis for race relations in the nation is not hopeful" (p. 233). In his insightful but pessimistic account of the "Negro revolution," Killian similarly warns "there is no way out" of the racial crisis that confronts us. Citing the destructive nature of American racism as a basis, he grimly predicts that white Americans "are not likely to make the sacrifices needed to change the fact that America is still a white man's society" (1968:xv).

As though to confirm the gloomy findings of attitude surveys

According to Armendáriz, the following figures are representative wherever Mexican-Americans are concentrated in a population:

In the City of Los Angeles, where we find the largest concentration of Mexican Americans in the world, the top fifteen industries hired only 9.7% Mexican Americans. Of these, only 4% have been hired in white-collar jobs; 68.3% of these were in the lower wage scales and clerical jobs.

In the great State of Texas, where 16% of the total population according to the 1960 census is Mexican American, only 4.7% are white-collar workers; 80% of these are in the lower wage scale and clerical jobs.

The Texas Advisory Committee to the Civil Rights Commission reports that in three of the largest corporations around a certain city with heavy concentration of Mexican American population and a large number of government contracts, out of a total of 1,350 persons employed, only nine are Mexican American.

Large percentages of Mexican American families live in poverty and have an annual income under $3000. The numbers range from 86% in some counties of Texas, to 24% in some counties in California. [1967. 190–191.]

and impressionistic accounts, there is convincing evidence that discriminatory practices and attendant inequities have retained their support in the fabric of American life. From private clubs to occupations and industries, individuals continue to be excluded by virtue of their religious affiliations (Pettigrew, 1971). Moreover, the almost 400,000 American Indians who presently live on or adjacent to reservations still constitute the most severely disadvantaged minority group in the United States with respect to income, unemployment, and housing (Sorkin, 1969). Median Indian income falls far below the so-called poverty level; the figure being less than $1,600 per year (Burnette,

1971). And most obviously, perhaps, there is widespread discrimination based on race. As noted in the Report of the National Advisory Commission on Civil Disorders (1968), great numbers of nonwhite Americans still fail to receive the benefits of economic progress. Discrimination occurs in employment and education and is a fact of life in housing and the courts. While incomes of blacks fall far below those of whites, unemployment rates for blacks remain double the figure for whites. Blacks who find work continue to be concentrated in the lowest-skilled and lowest-paying positions in our society (Cook, 1970).

The Commission on the Cities in the 1970s in its visits to major American cities in 1971 found a worsening of the "shameful conditions of life in the cities" with respect to crime, disease, heroin addiction, and welfare rolls. According to findings of the Commission, though nonwhite Americans have made progress since 1960, they continue to lag discouragingly behind whites in important areas such as median income, education, unemployment, life expectancy, and infant mortality. What is more, American institutions—its corporations, courts, legislatures, schools, police, mayors, and banks—are increasingly being viewed as unresponsive to human needs and rapidly losing the confidence of the American people. Projecting on the basis of the 1970 census and more current trends, the Commission concludes that "most cities by 1980 will be preponderantly black and brown, and totally bankrupt" (p. 6).

SUMMARY AND CONCLUSION

Prejudice has severely impaired the operating effectiveness of our society—a society that claims to evaluate all of its members on the basis of achievement and universalism at the same time that it handicaps certain individuals strictly on the basis of their membership in a minority group. Thus, American minorities suffer the dysfunctional consequences of prejudice with respect to their ability to compete for class, status, and power, if not their mental health or their very existence as a group. But majority-group members suffer as well, for prejudice demands of them an expenditure of energy at the psychological level that could be more profitably directed toward self-interest in the direct pursuit of their important goals. Mechanisms of defense provide some comfort or security for an individual, but they often also detract from his larger, longer-term effectiveness. Moreover, since prejudice ordinarily affronts democratic standards of interpersonal conduct, it often serves as a basis for profound conflicts in our system of values and social structure, producing tensions and strains wherever they occur.

Despite convincing evidence to suggest the malignancy of prejudice—its costly and debilitating consequences—some soical scientists presently assert that prejudice can *no longer* be held accountable for the poverty, miseducation, and underemployment being experienced by the minority groups in our society. Their argument runs as follows: Though *initially* responsible for the problems of minorities, prejudice or racism of the majority is no longer to blame for such problems. The minority group is regarded as trapped in a self-feeding vicious circle of deprivation that is difficult if not impossible to reverse.

What is too little recognized by spokesmen for the foregoing viewpoint, however, is that prejudice also performs some important *positive functions* for certain groups in our society, and, in this sense, continues to be very much implicated in the inequities suffered by American minorities.

Following Merton's (1957) usage, we define *function* as a consequence that aids in the adjustment of a system. Also like Merton, we recognize a range of levels—personality, subgroup, culture, society—for which any item may have consequences. The central thesis of this work is that prejudice persists in our society because it continues to have adaptive gains for elements within the majority group and, secondarily, within the minority as well. It follows that we then can only reduce prejudice and attendant majority-minority inequities to the extent that we come to grips with the important functions that prejudice serves.

In line with our concept of prejudice, the two-fold purpose of the present work involves: (1) identifying and analyzing the range of important personality and social functions that prejudice performs, and (2) focusing on certain characteristics of American society that help to explain why prejudice continues to be functional.

It might reasonably be argued that a one-sided emphasis on the functions of prejudice to the exclusion of its dysfunctions could be employed to support a conservative ideological position, justifying a phenomenon that ought to be condemned and eliminated. Admittedly, there is always the danger that those who are wedded to the status quo will seize upon this analysis as an excuse to argue against full equality for American minorities. In a larger view, however, we note again that social science has previously given an imbalanced emphasis to the dysfunctions of prejudice—its debilitating and morally offensive consequences for the groups in our society. Judging by most sociological analyses, prejudice has absolutely no positive functions for anyone (Tumin, 1965). Such an emphasis has unfortunately not yielded an effective conception of the causes of prejudice in America. Moreover, as pointed out by Merton (1957) and more recently by Gans (1972), "functional analysis per se is ideologically neutral," though its implications may be employed to support or to rebut a particular political stance.

What do we mean by "prejudice"? As used here, we define prejudice as *interpersonal hostility which is directed against individuals based on their membership in a minority group.* This conception of prejudice is meant to focus our attention on negative feelings, beliefs, and action-tendencies that arise against human beings by virtue of the status they occupy or are perceived to occupy as members of a minority.

The nature of prejudice can be examined at the psychological level as *a negative attitude toward the members of a minority group*. As such, prejudice is a learned disposition consisting of (1) negative beliefs or stereotypes, (2) negative feelings or emotions, and (3) the tendency to discriminate.

From a sociological standpoint, prejudice can be regarded as *an element of the culture—the normative order—of the society in which its exists*. As a cultural phenomenon, prejudice is an enduring and widely shared characteristic of a society, being transmitted by its members from generation to generation, and receiving strong support in the form of custom or the enforcement of legal codes. In the history of American society, prejudice has been translated into *ideal norms* regarding the proper behavior of minorities in their dealings with members of the dominant group and prescribed *roles* which minority members were expected to play.

Despite a decline in the overall level of prejudice, the evidence is all too convincing that prejudice still has a tenacious hold on many members of American society, persisting at an alarmingly high level especially against such groups as blacks, Puerto Ricans, Mexican-Americans, American Indians, and Jews. The evidence from attitude surveys, impressionistic accounts, and statistical data indicate that majority Americans are not likely to make the sacrifices needed to produce equality for minority Americans.

In the next chapter, we begin our analysis by asking what the positive functions of prejudice for the personality of majority-group members are? In this regard, we focus upon (1) the displacement of aggression, (2) the protection of self-esteem, and (3) the reduction of uncertainty. Chapter 3 explores the social functions of prejudice for the majority group —those consequences of an economic or a political nature that aid in the maintenance of the majority group *qua* group. In particular, we shall address ourselves to (1) the maintenance of occupation status, (2) the performance of unpleasant or low-paying jobs, and (3) the maintenance of power. In Chapter 4, we turn our attention to secondary gains and special opportunities that exist in a minority group by virtue of the hostility that confronts it. Our analysis is directed to the following functions of prejudice: (1) the reduction of competition, (2) the maintenance of solidarity, and (3) the reduction of uncertainty. In the final chapter of the book, we examine certain sociocultural characteristics that may account for the functional nature of prejudice in our society and, on this basis, discuss prospects for the reduction of prejudice.

chapter two

PERSONALITY FUNCTIONS OF PREJUDICE FOR THE MAJORITY GROUP

Sartre once wrote, "If the Jew did not exist, the anti-Semite would invent him" (1965:13). Nowhere can the functional nature of prejudice be seen more clearly than in the gains that accrue to the personality of a majority-group member who harbors negative feelings, beliefs, and action-tendencies regarding a minority. In its *ego-defensive* consequences, prejudice provides a safe outlet for displaced aggression and aids in the maintenance or enhancement of self-esteem. With reference to its *knowledge* function, prejudice is capable of reducing the myriad uncertainties, both emotional as well as cognitive, to which all of us are exposed in the course of our everyday affairs (Katz, 1960).

To be sure, such payoffs have their costs as well; for instance, the defensive energy expended by a prejudiced individual to safeguard his self-image may jeopardize his chances to find a long-term, more effective adaptation. In this connection, one is reminded of a student so busy convincing himself of his superiority that he doesn't study and fails his examinations.

Moreover, the use of prejudice as a factor in interpersonal perception will likely give a distorted and unrealistic view of others, a view that can mislead an individual seeking to fulfill his goals.

Yet the immediate positive functions of prejudice for the maintenance of the personality of a majority-group member can hardly be exaggerated. Prejudice sustains the personality in the face of deprivation or external threat and helps to structure a highly complex, otherwise chaotic, social environment. We cannot understand the nature of prejudice without taking account of such personality functions. A good place to begin is to examine the nature of displaced aggression.

DISPLACEMENT OF AGGRESSION

There is an old story, which has probably replayed countless times throughout history, concerning a frustrated, belittled, and hostile worker who submits passively to the daily indignities dished out by his tyrannical boss, while he "takes it out" on his wife by shouting obscenities or periodically beating her. This is a clear-cut example of what is known as *displaced aggression*. The frustrations imposed by a powerful figure (in this case, a tyrannical boss) creates feelings of intense anger and hostility in the worker, which he safely displaces or redirects to an innocent target, his wife. To the extent that she takes the blame for a matter not of her making, the worker's wife becomes a scapegoat for her husband.

Frustration and Aggression

In *Frustration and Aggression,* Dollard, Doob, Miller, Mowrer, and Sears are convinced that *aggression is the inevitable consequence of frustration:*

More specifically the proposition is that the occurrence of aggressive behavior always presupposes the existence of frustration and, contrariwise, that the existence of frustration always leads to some form of aggression. From the point of view of daily observation, it does not seem unreasonable to assume that aggressive behavior of the usually recognized varieties is always traceable to and produced by some form of frustration. But it is by no means so immediately evident that, whenever frustration occurs, aggression of some kind and in some degree will inevitably result. In many adults and even children, frustration may be followed so promptly by an apparent acceptance of the situation and readjustment thereto that one looks in vain for the relatively gross criteria ordinarily thought of as characterizing aggressive action. It must be kept in mind, however, that one of the earliest lessons human beings learn as a result of social living is to suppress and restrain their overtly aggressive reactions. This does not mean, however, that such reaction tendencies are thereby annihilated; rather it has been found that, although these reactions may be temporarily compressed, delayed, disguised, displaced, or otherwise deflected from their immediate and logical goal, they are not destroyed. [1939:1–2.]

Whether or not frustration and aggression are inextricably bound together, we have compelling reason to believe that the myriad frustrations of everyday life tend to increase aggressive motivation (Henry and Short, 1954; Palmer, 1960; Rule and Percival, 1971). Just as clearly, hostility or aggression cannot always be directed against the true source of a frustration, for the source may be vague and difficult to identify or much too powerful for safe attack. In order to blow off steam, then, an individual who has experienced frustration may attempt to locate a more vulnerable and visible enemy against whom his hostility can be directed with relative impunity.

Minorities as Scapegoats

Lacking the resources for retaliation, American minorities have traditionally served as targets for the displaced aggression of the majority group. In this regard, blacks have made especially desirable scapegoats, for not only were they powerless to strike back but they had adequate visibility as well. Until 1930, for example, the frequency with which blacks in the South were lynched increased as the value of Southern cotton declined (Hovland and Sears, 1970). To blow off the steam that accompanies increased frustration, Southern whites apparently found it useful to focus the blame for their economic hardships on blacks, though by no stretch of the imagination could blacks have been responsible for the price of cotton or the level of economic depression in the South. For similar reasons, the Depression of the 1930s saw the birth of 114 organizations that spent their time and money in spreading anti-Semitism (Rose, 1958). And, on a wider scale, the Depression period brought a substantial increase in nativist activity aimed at the total exclusion of potential immigrants as well as the wholesale deportation of recent arrivals. As before, the newcomers were blamed for all of America's economic ills (LaGumina, 1973).

Early experimental evidence for the existence of displaced aggression was provided by Miller and Bugelski (1948), who required thirty-one men in a vocational training camp to take a series of lengthy and difficult examinations that prevented them from visiting the local movie house where the most interesting event of the week was taking place. Both before and after these exams were administered by Miller and Bugelski, they measured the attitudes of their subjects toward Japanese and Mexicans. This was done by having the men check a list of ten desirable and ten undesirable traits as being either present or absent in the average Mexican or Japanese. The results of the study were as expected by the investigators: the men regarded Mexicans and Japanese less favorably after the frustrating examination

The frustration-aggression hypothesis (Dollard et al., 1939) has guided much of the research into the social psychology of aggression conducted over the past few decades. Despite the criticism that has been leveled against it, this hypothesis continues to provide a valuable focal point for the study of various forms of aggression including prejudice. However, most social scientists presently agree that frustration is not the only nor the most powerful cause of aggression (Green, 1972).

The scapegoat or displaced aggression hypothesis has additional problems, though it too has been the subject of much research. As Berkowitz (1962) reminds us, aggression is not always displaced, but is frequently directed against the perceived source of frustration. Displacement of aggression may be more likely to occur, however, if the frustrator is powerful or difficult to locate (Williams, 1947) or when the frustration is accidental, beyond the control of the frustrator, or carried out in a socially acceptable manner (Burnstein and Worchel, 1962; Geen, 1972). Moreover, the weakest target is not always the recipient of displaced aggression. Frequently, the scapegoat may be selected for his similarity to the actual source of the frustration (Berkowitz, 1962). The scapegoat may also be relatively strong, if he is chosen in order to restore self-esteem to the victim of frustration (White and Lippitt, 1960). Finally, displaced aggression does not always occur in experiments designed to test for its presence (Rosnow, Holz, and Levin, 1966; Stagner and Congdon, 1955) and may be associated with certain personality types (Adorno et al., 1950).

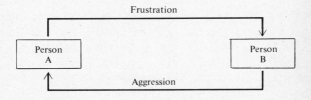

Figure 2–1. The relationship between frustration and aggression

The scapegoat phenomenon is clearly represented in the meaning of the bumper sticker below that supposedly appeared during the 1973 energy crisis:

HELP END THE ENERGY CRISIS:

BURN A JEW

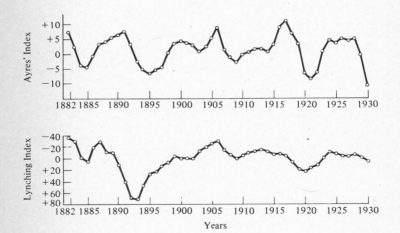

Figure 2–2.   Relation of lynchings to a composite economic index (Ayres)

Source: Carl I. Hovland and Robert R. Sears   1970   "Minor Studies of Aggression: Correlation of Lynchings with Economic Indices." *Journal of Psychology* (Winter): 304

than prior to it. Specifically, from pretest to posttest, there was a significant decrease in the number of favorable items checked and a slight increase in the number of negative items checked.

The findings of Miller and Bugelski have been replicated several times since 1948, either by means of paper-and-pencil questionnaires in which subjects express their aggressive feelings (Cowen, Landes, and Schaet, 1959) or, more behaviorally, as the tendency of a subject to administer an intense electrical shock to another naive subject (Holmes, 1972). At the same time, social scientists have taken note of the fact that frustration cannot always be accurately conceptualized or measured in absolute terms. George Bernard Shaw recognized this when he astutely noted, "It is not enough to succeed. One's friends must fail." Hence, the notion of *relative deprivation,* a concept that focuses on the level of achievement attained by an individual *relative* to the standard that he employs as a basis of comparison.

Relative Deprivation and Prejudice

Not all forms of frustration are obvious. As a result, the concept of relative deprivation has been useful for the purpose of identifying frustration and its sources. For instance, Bettelheim and Janowitz (1964) uncovered no relationship between income level or socioeconomic status and intensity of anti-Semitism, but found that downwardly mobile men—individuals who had moved lower in terms of socioeconomic status by comparison with their previous civilian employment—expressed greater hostility against Jews than did men stable with respect to socioeconomic status. For these men, loss of occupational status apparently constituted a frustration sufficiently intense to generate considerable ethnic hostility.

More recent reseach has indicated that feelings of relative deprivation are not necessarily indicated by conventional measures of frustration. In a particular survey, for instance, it was found that George Wallace supporters in the presidential election of 1968 were surprisingly well-off: more specifically, individuals having annual family incomes between $7,500 and $10,000 were much more likely to support Wallace than those who had family incomes under $5,000 (Pettigrew, Riley, and Vanneman, 1972). Yet frustration was very much a factor among Wallace supporters. In the first place, Wallace-ites tended to have *status inconsistency* (high income but low education), a condition thought to produce much psychological stress and tension (Eitzen, 1970). Moreover, Wallace supporters clearly tended to feel relatively deprived in social-class terms when they compared the economic gains of their group— the working class—to those of white-collar workers. Thus, Wallace-ites more than supporters of Nixon or Humphrey would agree that "in spite of what some people say, the condition of the average man is getting worse not better." In reference to George Wallace's constituents, Pettigrew, Riley, and Vanneman wrote, "We had a picture of solid, fairly comfortable, fairly well-educated persons displaying psychological characteristics—political alienation, fear, distrust, racial bias—that generally are found most intensely among the worst-educated and most poverty-stricken segments of the population" (1972:49).

PROTECTION OF SELF-ESTEEM

Though prejudice against the members of a minority group may often occur as a result of a need to get rid of the aggression that accompanies frustration, prejudice can have a more profound and complex meaning for the personality of a prejudiced person. It is a method of defending self-image, whereby, for the majority member, a minority group becomes a *negative reference group,* or a point of comparison against which the values, abilities, or performances of the majority member can be regarded as superior.

Social Comparison and Self-Esteem

Indeed, some psychologists have argued that virtually all displaced aggression is of an ego-defensive nature, having as its primary objective the restoration of an individual's self-esteem or status (White and Lippitt, 1960). This may be particularly true with respect to the development of prejudice. By the use of a minority as a negative reference group, an individual need not acknowledge truths about himself or about threatening aspects of his environment. As noted by Daniel Katz, "When we cannot admit to ourselves that we have deep feelings of inferiority we may project those feelings onto some convenient minority group and bolster our egos by attitudes of superiority toward this underprivileged group" (1960:172).

Several experimental studies have yielded support for the view that individuals employ negative reference groups in an effort to maintain or restore self-esteem. In this regard, Hakmiller (1966) reported that subjects exposed to a high-threat condition (having been given negative information about themselves) were more likely than subjects in a low-threat condition to make *downward comparisons* with individuals regarded as clearly inferior with respect to the performance being compared. For Hakmiller, this finding reflects the operation of defensive social comparison, "the function of comparison in this situation of sustaining or reasserting the favorability of the individual's self-regard" (1966:37). In a more recent study, Wilson and Benner (1971) set out to examine the notion that individuals having high self-esteem would choose a "comparison other" to maximize the information they obtain about themselves whereas individuals who have low self-esteem would seek instead to avoid a potentially threatening comparison. After receiving their scores on a "leadership test," Wilson and Benner's subjects were given the opportunity to compare their leadership ability with that of another student. The expectation was clear: subjects with low self-esteem should want to compare themselves with someone lower in ability and should avoid a high-scoring "comparison other." Results of the study by Wilson and Benner tended to support their prediction. In a public condition, significantly more high self-esteem males chose the highest scorer as a "comparison other" than did low self-esteem males. For female subjects, self-esteem influenced choices of "comparison other" in a private condition, where sex-related competition was minimal.

If defensive social comparison requires the availability of an "inferior" reference group, then the presence of a negatively regarded minority group such as blacks, Puerto Ricans, Mexican-Americans, or Jews may represent an ideal situation for a majority-group member. Social scientists have long stressed the importance of excessive concern with the attainment of higher status as a cause of prejudice (Blalock, 1967; Kaufman, 1957; Williams, 1964). Dollard, in his perceptive analysis of life in a small Southern town, clearly identified the manner in which white southerners gained status and self-esteem by virtue of their position in the traditional pattern of race relations found in the deep South:

> In the North a man may have a prestige position because he has money, or is learned, or is old; the novelty in the South is that one has prestige solely because one is white. The gain here is very simple. It consists in the fact that a member of the white caste has an automatic right to demand forms of behavior from Negroes which serve to increase his own self-esteem. To put it another way, it consists of an illumination of the image of the self, an expansive feeling of being something special and valuable. It might be compared to the illusion of greatness that comes with early stages of alcoholization, except that prestige is not an illusion, but a steadily repeated fact. [1937:174.]

The phenomenon of defensive social comparison with a minority-group member was experimentally explored by Levin (1969) who exposed his subjects, a group of 180 college students, either to relative deprivation or to relative satisfaction regarding their performance on a bogus test of achievement during a regular class period. In the relative-deprivation condition, the students were led to believe their examination scores fell far below that of "the average student in similar groups of undergraduates." By contrast, students in the relative-satisfaction condition were told their scores were substantially higher than that of "the average student." Immediately after receiving their examination grades, all subjects answered the following paper-and-pencil measure of prejudice against Puerto Ricans:

> Directions: Place an "X" in one position between the adjectives of each scale (e.g., __ : __ : __) to indicate how well these adjectives apply in general to Puerto Ricans. Your evaluation should reflect what you believe *many* of the members of this particular group tend to be (what the average Puerto Rican is like), and *not* necessarily what 100% of them are.

PUERTO RICANS

	1	2	3	4	5	6	7	
reputable	__ :	__ :	__ :	__ :	__ :	__ :	__	disreputable
knowledgeable	__ :	__ :	__ :	__ :	__ :	__ :	__	ignorant
intelligent	__ :	__ :	__ :	__ :	__ :	__ :	__	stupid
industrious	__ :	__ :	__ :	__ :	__ :	__ :	__	lazy
kind	__ :	__ :	__ :	__ :	__ :	__ :	__	cruel
clean	__ :	__ :	__ :	__ :	__ :	__ :	__	dirty
straightforward	__ :	__ :	__ :	__ :	__ :	__ :	__	sly
reliable	__ :	__ :	__ :	__ :	__ :	__ :	__	unreliable

Levin found that exposure to relative deprivation yielded a more negative evaluation of Puerto Ricans (as indicated by the tendency to place a check mark closer to negative adjectives) than did relative satisfaction, but only among certain subjects. Specifically, subjects affected by relative deprivation were *relative evaluators,* individuals who tended to rely heavily on a social frame of reference for the measurement of success in fulfilling their goals. These were persons who, as indicated by their scores on a paper-and-pencil measure of relative evaluation, were likely to evaluate their personal performances relative to the productivity or achievement of other persons or groups. By contrast, subjects who did not become more prejudiced under relative deprivation were *self-evaluators,* individuals who relied upon their other personal performances, past or present, as a standard of comparison (i.e., personal improvement). A questionnaire survey of the students who participated in this study revealed that relative evaluators scored higher than self-evaluators on measures of authoritarianism, conflict, and competitiveness. Moreover, as compared with self-evaluators relative evaluators were significantly more likely to prefer careers in profit-making and money-oriented occupations. To summarize these findings, then, prejudice against Puerto Ricans increased under relative deprivation, but only among individuals initially predisposed toward making social

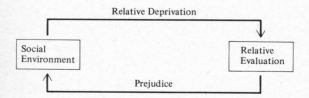

Figure 2–3. The mediating influence of relative evaluation on the relationship between relative deprivation and prejudice

comparisons and employing negative reference groups or individuals in order to maintain or bolster their self-image.

The Authoritarian Personality

The foregoing conception is not without precedence in the literature of social science. During the 1940s, at a time when fascism and anti-Semitism were of major concern to social scientists and laymen alike, Adorno et al. (1950) set out to examine systematically the possible existence of a deep-lying personality predisposition for directing aggression to minority groups. In their research, Adorno and his collaborators amassed a good deal of evidence for the presence of an *authoritarian personality structure,* a configuration of functionally interrelated personality characteristics in which prejudice plays an important part.

The symptoms of authoritarianism were identified by the F (potentiality for fascism) Scale, a series of opinion items to which individuals were asked to express their agreement or disagreement. Below are the nine characteristics in the authoritarian syndrome and an item from the F Scale to illustrate each one. An affirmative response to any item indicates authoritarianism.

1. *Conventionalism.* This characteristic involves a rigid commitment to conventional, middle-class values and goals; a disposition to feel anxious by the very expectation that such values and goals might be violated by others.
   Example Item: "Obedience and respect for authority are the most important virtues children should learn."

2. *Authoritarian Submission.* This involves an exaggerated need to submit to moral authorities of the in-group.
   Example Item: "Young people sometimes get rebellious ideas, but as they grow up they ought to get over them and settle down."

3. *Authoritarian Aggression*. This is the tendency to condemn and punish individuals who are suspected of violating conventional, middle-class values.

   Example Item: "Homosexuals are hardly better than criminals and ought to be severely punished."

4. *Anti-Intraception*. This entails opposition to subjective, imaginative, "tender-minded" phenomena.

   Example Item: "When a person has a problem or worry, it is best for him not think about it, but to keep busy with more cheerful things."

5. *Superstition and Stereotypy*. Both of these involve a narrowness of consciousness. In the case of superstitiousness, there is a tendency to perceive responsibility for the individual's fate in outside forces beyond his control. With respect to stereotypy, the tendency is to think in rigid, oversimplified categories.

   Example Item: "Some people are born with an urge to jump from high places."

6. *Power and Toughness*. This characteristic includes an alignment of the individual with power figures; a preoccupation with strength versus weakness, dominance versus submission, and an exaggerated assertion of power and toughness.

   Example Item: "People can be divided into two distinct classes: the weak and the strong."

7. *Destructiveness and Cynicism*. This involves a generalized resentment and hostility toward humans.

   Example Item: "Human nature being what it is, there will always be war and conflict."

8. *Projectivity*. This characteristic entails the belief that wild and dangerous events occur in the world, a projection onto the external world of unconscious emotional impulses.

   Example Item: "Wars and social troubles may some day be ended by an earthquake or flood that will destroy the whole world."

9. *Sex*. This involves an exaggerated concern with the sexual behavior of other people.

Example Item: "The wild sex life of the old Greeks and Romans was tame compared to some of the goings-on in this country, even in places where people might least expect it."

According to Adorno et al., the origin of the authoritarian personality is located in the early socialization experiences of the child, particularly, in harsh and punitive forms of discipline and clearly defined family roles. The authoritarian child is expected to be weak and to submit to the desires of his parents; the parents, in turn, assume a dominant posture in their relations with the child. As a result, an authoritarian child makes only a superficial identification with his parents, actually harboring much latent hostility and resentment toward them. The outcome of such childhood experiences has relevance for an understanding of prejudice: the authoritarian finally comes to treat others in the manner that his parents treated him. As an adult, he maintains a general contempt for the allegedly inferior and weak members of his society; he comes to despise such diverse groups as blacks, foreigners, Puerto Ricans, Catholics, and Jews. In this manner, the authoritarian bolsters his self-esteem, avoids painful truths about himself, and clarifies his perceptions of the world.

REDUCTION OF UNCERTAINTY

To this point, we have examined the ego-defensive functions of prejudice for the personality of a majority-group member. We turn our attention now to the part played by prejudice in structuring the perceived world of the majority-group member. We begin with the mass media.

One of the most widely employed concepts of prejudice can be found in the work of the "Berkeley Group" which produced *The Authoritarian Personality* (1950). Several hundred research projects, many focusing on the relationship between authoritarianism and prejudice, have followed the publication of the original work, and the body of research continues to grow. At the same time, however, critics of this work have focused upon several of its major deficiencies and limitations. We shall review a few of these here.

1. *Only the politically reactionary segment of authoritarianism was studied.* Research into authoritarianism was conducted at a time when fascism was of major concern to both social scientists as well as laymen. As a result, authoritarianism became equated with commitment to fascist ideology and anti-Semitism. As Rokeach (1960) subsequently determined, however, authoritarianism may also be found among radicals, liberals, and middle-of-the-roaders.

2. *A tendency toward acquiescence can partially account for the relationship of authoritarianism to prejudice.* The F Scale was constructed so that agreement with any of its items would indicate authoritarianism. In order to obtain a low authoritarianism score, then, an individual would have to disagree with the statements in the F Scale. However, social scientists have discovered the presence of so-called yeasayers and naysayers, individuals who tend to agree or disagree with any statement on any scale, regardless of its specific content (Couch and Keniston, 1960). Therefore, agreement with F Scale items may indicate a general disposition to agree as well as (or instead of) general authoritarianism.

3. *A third variable may partially explain the apparent relationship between authoritarianism and prejudice.* When the effect of such variables as "concern with achieving high status" (Golden, 1974; Kaufman, 1957) or "anomie" (Srole, 1956) is held constant, the relationship between authoritarianism and prejudice diminishes.

By the use of a statistical procedure known as partial correlation, Kaufman (1957) examined the intensity of the relationship between authoritarianism and prejudice both before and after he controlled for [or held constant] the influence of status concern. The original correlation of .53 [fairly strong] between authoritarianism and prejudice [before controlling for status concern] dropped sharply to .12 when the effect of status concern was held constant. As a result, Kaufman suggested that the correlation between authoritarianism and prejudice can be explained at least in part by the mutual association of these variables with status concern. Also on the basis of partial correlation, Srole (1956) similarly concluded that anomie [a psychological state characterized by personal disorganization and alienation from group life] may account for much of the relationship between authoritarianism and prejudice.

4. *The Authoritarian Personality fails to give adequate recognition to cultural forms of prejudice.* For the authors of *The Authoritarian Personality,* prejudice is psychologically pathological. Yet regional and societal differences in prejudice occur that probably cannot be explained on the basis of authoritarian predispositions. If, for example, the residents of Georgia are found to be more prejudiced against blacks than are the residents of Rhode Island, this does not necessarily mean that they are more "authoritarian." Different cultural norms may be operating to produce differences in prejudice. Any adequate conception of prejudice must therefore consider social, structural, and cultural differences as well (Simpson and Yinger, 1972).

Note: Many of the deficiencies of the original version of authoritarianism can be overcome. For example, revised versions of the F Scale have been constructed to minimize the influence of acquiescence (Christie, Havel, and Seidenberg, 1958) and to measure left-wing authoritarianism (Rokeach, 1960). There is also growing realization that authoritarianism is but one of the many factors associated with prejudice—a factor that interacts with sociocultural variables to determine the nature of intergroup relations in a society.

Mass Media Stereotypes

In 1946, Berelson and Salter identified the stereotyped portrayals of minority characters in short stories as a convenient method of "getting the character across" to an audience (1946: 187). As later explained by O'Hara, the prejudicial treatment of characters serves to frame a mass communication message in terms that are meaningful to the members of American society:

> It enables the mass communicator to frame his messages with the least amount of lost motion, and it enables the receiver to comprehend what is being communicated with equal speed and facility. He is given situations and characters that have become familiar to him. . . . There is, therefore, little lost motion on either side of the fence. [1961:194.]

Nowhere is there a better example of the effective use of stereotypes to facilitate characterization than in the "Amos and Andy Show," a popular radio and television program that for decades routinely depicted derogatory but *familiar* images of black Americans. In *Confessions of a White Racist,* Larry King analyzes the characterizations of "The Amos and Andy Show":

> Who does not readily recognize the white man's nigger as represented by the cast? Lawyer Calhoun pretended to a literacy so obviously impossible in a black man that he could only spout quasi-legalisms in the most unintelligible terms; Andy was a *cum laude* graduate of the School of Memorable Malapropisms as well as an inordinately sly dog among coveys of loose black ladies; "Lightnin' " from his office-boy station was so lazy he only reluctantly expended the energy required to breathe; George (Kingfish) Stevens embodied the sum

qualities of all "bad niggers" everywhere—a con man who naturally preferred ill-gotten gains to honest labors, a philanderer even under the cold Black Maternalism eye of wife Sapphire, a circus nigger who dug parading in colorful lodge uniforms while pretending to ludicrous titles. Among regulars on the show only Amos was a good nigger, a white nigger, a nigger who might be trusted in the presence of the white man's money or his sister. He alone had a steady job or wanted one; he sometimes tried to persuade his black brothers to higher moral paths; he even paid his bills and told his children bedtime stories. Yes, Amos was what all his brothers might have become if only the black man had not been famed for excesses of larceny or so few brains. [1969:5.]

The reliance of media stereotypes on the familiar and the simple can be seen in their portrayal of the linguistic difficulties of American minorities. For example, blacks have traditionally been depicted as indiscriminately substituting the "d" sound for "th." Thus, a black might be viewed as saying "dis" and "dat" as in "lift dat bale" or "dis is de place." In a similar way, the Mexican has been characterized as handicapped by his use of the double "e." A Mexican character might typically say "theenk" rather than "think"; "peenk" rather than pink. By contrast, the American Indian has been depicted as devoid of any English at all; his linguistic ability generally limited to "ugh," "kemo sabe," or some monosyllabic grunt.

The only exception to this rule is a line famed for its durability over the years. If you fall asleep during the Late Show and suddenly awaken to the words 'go in peace my son,' it is either an Indian chief bidding his son good-bye as the boy heads for college or a Roman Catholic priest forgiving Paul Newman or Steve McQueen for killing a hundred men in the preceding reel. [Deloria, 1970:37.]

Simplifying the World

Just as it works in the context of mass communication, so prejudice operates in the lives of many persons to "define the situation," provide order and clarity, and reduce the cognitive and emotional uncertainties of everyday experiences. Every individual has the need "to give adequate structure to his universe" (Katz, 1969:170). How this is done may vary a good deal from one individual to another.

One thing is clear, however: individuals do not always define one another exclusively on the basis of cues that they receive in social interaction. Undoubtedly, there are times when interpersonal attitudes must be formed in the absence of detailed information about another person. For instance, a prospective employer might have to form a judgment of the abilities of a job applicant after having interviewed him for only a short period of time.

Culturally supported prejudices provide ready-made expectations in terms of which individuals can be categorized. What people often do is to fill the gap in their knowledge of others with oversimplified and distorted preconceptions, many of which are based upon group membership. Thus, a prospective employer who knows little about a black job applicant, save from his limited contact in an interview situation, might use an anti-black stereotype in order to form a conclusion regarding the applicant's abilities (Katz, 1960).

While stereotyped categories narrow the amount of information necessary for action to occur, they also expand the scope of available information (Ehrlich, 1972). Thus, the prospective employer who evaluates an applicant on the basis of his "blackness" immediately gains much information about characteristics that the applicant presumably shares with other members of his race. This is what author Langston Hughes

(Chapman, 1968) had in mind for his fictional character, Simple, when he wrote:

". . . being white and curious, my boss keeps asking me just what does THE Negro want. Yesterday he tackled me during the coffee break, talking about THE Negro. He always says 'the Negro,' as if there was not 50–11 different kinds of Negroes in the U.S.A.," complained Simple. "My boss says, 'Now that you-all have got the Civil Rights Bill and the Supreme Court, Adam Powell in Congress, Ralph Bunche in the United Nations, and Leontyne Price singing in the Metropolitan Opera, plus Dr. Martin Luther King getting the Nobel Prize, what more do you want? I am asking you, just what does THE Negro want?" 'I am not the Negro,' I says. I am *me*.' [1968:106–107.]

Intolerance of Ambiguity

Prejudiced persons seem to be especially intolerant of cognitive and emotional ambiguities (Martin and Westie, 1959; Steiner and Johnson, 1963; Triandis and Triandis, 1972). According to Adorno et al. (1950), this aversion of prejudiced individuals is a generalization of their intolerance of the affectual ambivalence that exists when both love and hate are felt for a parent. Prejudiced persons desire absolute and unequivocal feelings about themselves and others; aided by a series of stereotyped polarities—black versus white, strong versus weak, hero versus villain—they suppress awareness of their own weaknesses and the weaknesses of their parents. Instead, their aggression is externalized. Members of the majority group are glorified and idealized, whereas culturally designated outgroups become targets for displaced hostility.

As adults, prejudiced individuals may be inaccurate *role*

takers, persons who are not capable of accurately estimating qualities of others from cues given in interactional settings. In this connection, Scodel and Mussen (1953) instructed pairs of strangers consisting of an authoritarian and a nonauthoritarian subject to discuss together several topics related to mass communication and then to estimate how they thought the subject with whom they had been interacting would respond to a series of attitude questions. The authoritarian subjects tended to perceive their nonauthoritarian peer as holding attitudes and personality characteristics similar to their own, whereas the nonauthoritarian subjects were better able to judge their peer accurately in terms of attitudes and personality. Similarly, Koenig and King (1962) found that students opposed to racial integration were less accurate in predicting the responses of others on campus than were students who expressed attitudes favorable to racial integration.

Experimental evidence for the presence of extreme intolerance of ambiguity in prejudiced persons was uncovered by Block and Block (1951), who tested sixty-five college students over one hundred trials as follows: Each subject was placed in a darkened room where he was asked to view a pinpoint of light until he saw it move and to estimate the distance that the light had traveled. Actually, these subjects were exposed to the "autokinetic phenomenon": the pinpoint of light was in fact stationary, but it gave the illusion of movement when viewed in a totally darkened room. Block and Block reported that students who had scored high on the Ethnocentrism Scale—a measure of general prejudice—were quicker than those who scored low on this scale to establish a norm for themselves regarding the movement of the light. More specifically, the prejudiced or ethnocentric subjects quickly reported the light as moving in a constant direction and to a constant number of inches from one trial to another; whereas, the subjects low in prejudice could bettter tolerate not having a clear-cut answer and took much longer to establish a norm regarding the movement of the light.

Rokeach (1952) similarly found that very prejudiced subjects were afraid to admit defeat when confronted with the challenging task of correctly matching names with the faces of strangers. Whereas prejudiced subjects made numerous erroneous guesses, subjects with less prejudice more often admitted being confused and were less willing to take wild guesses.

SUMMARY AND CONCLUSION

Nowhere can the functional nature of prejudice be seen more clearly than in the gains that accrue to the personality of a majority-group member who harbors negative feelings, beliefs, and action-tendencies regarding a minority. In particular, prejudice can be employed to displace aggression, protect self-esteem, and reduce uncertainties.

There is compelling reason to believe that the myriad frustrations of everyday life tend to increase aggressive motivation. Just as clearly, aggression cannot always be directed against the true source of frustration, for the source may be vague and difficult to identify or too powerful for safe attack. In order to blow off steam, then, an individual who has experienced frustration may try to locate a more vulnerable and visible enemy against whom his hostility can be directed with relative impunity. Lacking the resources for retaliation, American minorities have frequently served as targets for the *displaced aggression* of the majority group.

Though prejudice against the members of a minority group may occur as a result of a need to get rid of the aggression that accompanies frustration, prejudice can also have a more profound and complex meaning for the personality of a prejudiced person. It is a method of defending self-image, whereby a minority group becomes a *negative reference group* for the majority member—a point of comparison against which the opinions, abilities, or performances of the majority member can be regarded as superior.

Some psychologists have argued that virtually all displaced aggression is actually of an ego-defensive nature, having as its primary objective the restoration of an individual's self-esteem or status. By using a minority group as a negative reference group, an individual need not acknowledge truths about himself or about threatening aspects of his environment.

There may be certain individuals who are especially pre-disposed toward making social comparisons and employing negative reference groups in order to maintain or to bolster their self-image. During the 1940s, a group of social scientists set out to examine the possible existence of a deep-lying personality predisposition for directing aggression to minority groups. They amassed a good deal of evidence for the presence of an *authoritarian personality structure,* a syndrome of functionally interrelated personality characteristics in which prejudice plays an important part. As a result of harsh and punitive forms of discipline in early socialization, the authoritarian personality comes to have a general contempt for the allegedly inferior and weak members of his society and in the process bolsters his self-esteem and avoids painful truths about himself.

Aside from its ego-defensive functions as discussed above, prejudice also plays a part in structuring the perceived world of the majority-group member. Prejudice operates in the lives of majority-group members to define the situation, provide order and clarity, and reduce the cognitive and emotional uncertainties of everyday experiences. Culturally supported prejudices provide ready-made expectations in terms of which individuals can easily be categorized.

Prejudiced individuals may be incapable of accurately estimating qualities of others from the cues given in interactional settings and seem to be especially intolerant of cognitive and emotional ambiguities.

In the next chapter, we again find ourselves addressing the question of whether and how prejudice is functional, but at an entirely different level. This time, we turn our attention to the social functions of prejudice.

chapter three

SOCIAL FUNCTIONS OF PREJUDICE FOR THE MAJORITY GROUP

Prejudice may be understood, in part, as an expression of latent forces that operate in order to fulfill the psychological needs of prejudiced individuals. As suggested in the last chapter, these needs may involve the displacement of aggression, the protection of self-esteem, or the reduction of cognitive and emotional uncertainties.

Personality functions of prejudice are important psychologically, but we must also examine the *social* functions of prejudice for the majority group—those consequences of a political or an economic nature that aid in the maintenance of the majority group *qua* group and of its advantaged position in a society. Unlike their personality counterparts, these social functions require the presence of hostility in the action-tendency component of prejudice that becomes translated into actual discrimination. Therefore, negative feelings or beliefs regarding a minority are relevant only in so far as they lead a majority-group member also to accord differential treatment to individuals on the basis of their minority status. Specifically, we address ourselves now to the consequences of prejudice for (1) the maintenance of occupational status, (2) the performance of unpleasant or low-paying jobs, and (3) the maintenance of power.

MAINTENANCE OF OCCUPATIONAL STATUS

Intergroup hostility tends to increase as competition for scarce resources becomes more intense. Sherif and his collaborators (1961) demonstrated the link between competition and intergroup hostility in a series of experiments that took place in an isolated summer camp for 11- and 12-year-old boys. After a period of time together, the boys attending the camp were separated into two groups and placed in different cabins. When each group of boys had developed a strong sense of group spirit and organization, Sherif arranged for a number of intergroup encounters—a tournament of competitive games such as football, baseball, tug-of-war, and a treasure hunt—in which one group could fulfill its goals only at the expense of the other group. Though the tournament began in a spirit of friendliness and good-natured rivalry, it soon became apparent that negative intergroup feelings were emerging on a large scale. The members of each group began to name-call their rivals, completely turning against members of the opposing group, even members whom they had selected as "best friends" upon first arriving at the camp.

Intergroup Competition

Sherif's findings shed light on the nature of majority-minority relations: When the maintenance or enhancement of the status of the majority group depends on the continued subordination of a minority, then we might expect that intergroup competition will become translated into prejudice. Indeed, some of the most visible benefits of prejudice for the majority group have a rational economic basis, occurring as the minority-group member attempts to secure a share of the scarce resources of his society. For example, there appears to be a direct relationship between the occurrence of anti-immigrant nativist activity and the incidence of economic depression. "The Native American party of the 1830s, the Know-Nothing Order of the 1850s, the American Protective Association in the last two decades of the nineteenth century, and the scores of anti-alien, one-hundred-percent-American groups in the 1930s—these all show the tendency to try to bolster a shaky economic situation by prejudice against recent immigrant groups" (Simpson and Yinger, 1972:116).

Large-scale economic problems such as the depressions of 1893 and 1907 served to solidify the opposition to further immigration from Italy, setting the stage for acceptance of stereotypes of Italians as "organ-grinders, paupers, slovenly ignoramuses, and so on" (LaGumina, 1973). Dollard (1938) has shown that local white Southerners became more hostile toward German newcomers to their town as economic conditions worsened and competition for jobs increased. In a similar way, Chinese immigrants to nineteenth-century America tended to be regarded as "honest," "industrious," and "peaceful" so long as jobs remained plentiful. But when the job market tightened and the Chinese began to seek work in mines, farming, domestic service, and factories, a dramatic increase in anti-Chinese sentiment emerged. They quickly became stereotyped as "dangerous," "deceitful," "vicious," and "clannish." Whites who felt themselves in competition for jobs accused the Chinese —just as they accused other immigrant groups—of undermining their standard of living (Sung, 1967).

According to van den Berghe, competition yields many of the conditions necessary for the development and maintenance of the prejudice associated with complex, industrialized societies that are based on large-scale manufacturing and a capitalist economy. Under such structural arrangements, the roles of majority and minority members are ill-defined and in a state of flux. Majority-group members feel themselves in direct competition with members of minority groups. There is concern for status, and antagonism prevails. "Competition, real or imaginary, for status, for jobs, for women, etc., or the threat of competition, poison race relations" (1966:60–61).

Such is not the case in traditional societies where a rather simple division of labor and an agricultural base require only minimal and latent forms of competitiveness, mobility, and status concern. Moreover, when it occurs in the traditional context, competitiveness rarely develops as a motivating force of everyday life and is generally built into the rigid status definitions of the system (e.g., castes).

Mexicans, American Indians, and the Acquisition of Land

In the history of American society, intergroup competition for scarce resources has often taken the form of organized efforts to secure land and extend political boundaries. Prejudice has played a central role in the acquisition of property for it has served to justify the ruthless, illegal tactics that were so frequently employed.

The experience of Mexican-Americans provides a case in point. After being stereotyped by Anglo-Americans as "treacherous, childlike, primitive, lazy, and irresponsible," Mexican-Americans found themselves manipulated by politicians, lawyers, and land-grabbers alike. Despite the 1848 Treaty of Guadalupe-Hidalgo, which guaranteed Mexicans the right of full citizenship, land-owning Mexican families found their titles in jeopardy and their land and cattle stolen or taken from them by fraud. Furthermore, they could not count on the courts for protection (Jacobs and Landau, 1971).

American Indians were severely mistreated at the hands of

land-hungry white Americans who eagerly accepted the view that Indians were "treacherous and cruel savages who could never be trusted." The negative stereotype served a purpose: As long as the Indians were needed for their agricultural expertise, their military assistance, or their skill as trappers, white Americans tended to regard them in a favorable light and to permit their culture to maintain itself; but when large-scale campaigns became directed toward securing the lands occupied and settled by Indians, the negative stereotype emerged in full force and the rules applicable to dealings between "civilized peoples of the world" were suspended. After all, if the central business of the Indian "savage" was to "torture" and "slay," then the central business of the white man must be gradually to eliminate the Indian "savage" (Jacobs and Landau, 1971).

In some cases, of course, the process of elimination was anything but gradual. By 1825, some thirteen thousand Cherokees maintained their homes in the southeastern region of the United States. They occupied seven million acres of land, owned prosperous farms, and were at peace. However, this situation was radically altered by the discovery of gold in the hills of Georgia. In order to gain possession of the rich Cherokee-owned lands, white Americans—with the help of the Georgia legislature, President Andrew Jackson, the United States Congress, the Supreme Court, and the military—found it "necessary" to drive the Cherokees beyond the Mississippi. In the Cherokee removal of 1838, Indians were rounded up and taken away, their homes were burned, their property was seized, many were herded into stockades, and thousands died (Berry, 1965).

Such thinking on the part of white Americans also led to the passage of the Dawes General Allotment Act of 1887, which took two-thirds (90 million acres) of the tribal lands previously granted to American Indians by treaty. "It does not take much sophistication to find a rationale for acquiring 90 million acres of land, especially when the owner cannot do anything to protect his property, and besides, wasn't even an American citizen" (Burnette, 1971).

Competition and Anti-black Prejudice

Anti-black sentiment in American society has run a similar course, generally becoming most intense among groups that have stood the most to lose from the equal treatment of blacks. It is not surprising that Southern white slave owners who enjoyed the economic and social rewards of the plantation sought to preserve the institution of slavery. What is less obvious, perhaps, is that the nearly three-fourths of the Southern whites who owned no slaves also profited from slavery (albeit indirectly) and, therefore, were no less willing to see it abolished. For the nonslaveholder, slavery was a method of limiting the competition from blacks and providing whites with highly visible membership in a superior caste (Stampp, 1956).

After the Civil War, the presence of whites in direct competition with ex-slaves for jobs assured the perpetuation of the myth that blacks were somehow innately ill-equipped for precisely the same skilled work they had competently performed before Emancipation (Bonacich, 1972; Harris, 1964). This was true, even though an absolute level of segregation and humiliation of blacks did not set in until the turn of the twentieth century, long after decades of racial conflict and competition led by a "relaxation of the opposition" to racism had established a firm hold on the character of our society (Woodward, 1955).

Dollard's (1937) "gains" theory of race relations represents an early attempt to understand the consequences of prejudice against blacks for the occupational status of white workers. In his classic study of a Southern community, Dollard observed that local whites gained occupationally from the presence of institutionalized forms of prejudice. Thus, as compared with their black counterparts in the community, whites in Southerntown generally got higher returns for their work and secured a disproportionately large share of goods and services.

The emotional impact of the fear of competition from blacks was clearly expressed in the following letter from a Southern white workingman who wrote at the turn of the twentieth century:

> All the genuine Southern people like the Negro as a servant, and so long as he remains the hewer of wood and carrier of water, and remains strictly in what we choose to call his place, everything is all right, but when ambition, prompted by real education, causes the Negro to grow restless and bestir himself to get out of that servile condition, then there is, or at least there will be, trouble, sure enough trouble, that all the great editors, parsons, and philosophers can no more check than they can now state the whole truth and nothing but the truth, about this all-absorbing, far-reaching miserable race question. There are those among Southern editors and other public men who have been shouting into the ears of the North for twenty-five years that education would solve the Negro question; there is not an honest, fearless, thinking man in the South but who knows that to be a bare-faced lie. Take a young Negro of little more than ordinary intelligence, even, get hold of him in time, train him thoroughly as to books, and finish him up with a good industrial education, send him out into the South with ever so good intentions both on the part of his benefactor and himself, send him to take my work away from me and I will kill him. [Franklin and Starr, 1967:25.]

In a more recent and more rigorous study of the relationship between minority subordination and majority occupational status, Glenn has similarly argued that a tradition of prejudice must be regarded as more than "merely a self-perpetuating carry-over from a past era which will certainly and rapidly disappear once the Myrdalian 'vicious circle' is broken" (1963: 447–448). In order to investigate his contention that the presence of self-interest continues to reinforce the existence of prejudice, Glenn investigated distributions of white income and occupational status for 151 large metropolitan areas during 1950, hypothesizing that occupational gains among whites would be higher where the relative size of the black population was greater. Glenn's findings generally confirmed his hypothesis. Whites did in fact experience important occupational gains from the continued subordination of large numbers of blacks, gains that included greater occupational prestige, better working conditions, as well as authority and independence on the job.

Examining data based on the 1960 census, Glenn (1966) similarly found that many whites living in Southern urbanized areas received important occupational benefits from the presence of a large and subordinated black population. Such benefits to whites in Southern localities with large black populations included more favorable occupational status, higher employment rates, and greater incomes than those obtained by whites in other Southern localities.

In light of the relationship between minority-group subordination and majority-group occupational status, it may not be surprising to learn that anti-black sentiment in contemporary American society continues to be most visible, if not most pronounced, among white working-class individuals, for these are the very individuals who are most anxious to protect their small amounts of power and status and *feel* most threatened by the possibility of racial equality. As Blauner (1972) suggests, 1.3 million white workers would have to be downgraded occupationally, in order to equalize the job distributions of blacks and whites. Moreover, racial equality would mean that the white working class—more than any other group in our society —would have to share its schools, neighborhoods, and political influence with blacks (Rossi, 1972). Such data go far to explain why working-class individuals are most likely to be attracted to groups such as the Ku Klux Klan (Vander Zanden, 1960) and to contribute in large numbers to a white backlash in the presence of civil rights activities (Rossi, 1972). As we shall see, however, prejudice against blacks may actually help affluent whites to depress the wages not only of black workers, but of their white counterparts as well. The attitudes of white workers toward blacks involve important occupational advantages, but they also involve misconceptions regarding the effects of inequality and numerous noneconomic factors in the lives of working-class whites.

The subordinate occupational status of nonwhite minorities can be seen in the following income data.

MEDIAN INCOME AND JOB DISTRIBUTION OF FULL-TIME MALE EMPLOYEES IN CENTRAL CITIES, 1967–1968

Occupation	Race	Median Income 1967	Job Distribution* 1968
Professional and managerial	W	$9542	30%
	NW	6208	9
Clerical and sales	W	6878	17
	NW	5515	12
Craftsmen and foremen	W	7545	21
	NW	5962	13
Operatives	W	6475	19
	NW	5414	32
Laborers (excluding farm)	W	5355	5
	NW	4492	17
Service workers (excluding private household)	W	5536	8
	NW	4159	17

* These figures indicate that, in the first category, 30 percent of all white males and 9 percent of all nonwhite males held professional or managerial positions in central cities in 1968, and so forth.

SOURCE: Adapted from Michael J. Flax 1971 *Blacks and Whites: An Experiment in Racial Indicators*. Washington, D.C.: The Urban Institute. P. 45

PERFORMANCE OF UNPLEASANT OR LOW-PAYING JOBS

To this point, we have been concerned with only a single dimension of the contribution to the majority group made by the presence of prejudice: As a result of their forced subordination, the absence of competition from members of minority groups helps to reserve the statuses with prestige and economic reward for members of the majority group. However, the flip side of this economic function must be given its due emphasis, namely, that prejudice justifies placing members of the minority in a position to serve the majority group, whether by taking low-paying jobs or by performing important tasks which the majority does not itself elect to perform.

The Jews in Medieval Europe

The history of the Jews provides an appropriate illustration. During the Middle Ages, European Jews were systematically excluded from such respectable activities as farming, owning land, and joining the guilds of craftsmen. Instead, Jews were generally restricted to the despised occupation of lending money at interest—an activity absolutely forbidden to the Christian majority on religious grounds—which was regarded as essential by the church and the nobility as a source of outside financing for building, farming, waging war, or engaging in political affairs. Powerless to protest or retaliate in an effective manner, Jews often played this necessary but stigmatizing role for the majority group.

In order to understand the reason why the Jews were the only group to perform the essential money-lending service, we must understand the attitude of the medieval church toward it. As viewed by the church, the lending of money for interest was sinful regardless of the amount of interest charged or the purpose for which money was borrowed. Thus, a Christian who today receives 5 percent interest on his savings account would have committed a mortal sin during the Middle Ages. As non-Christians, however, Jews were a different story altogether. In the view of the medieval church, Jews were already headed for hell; their participation in money lending could add little to the eternal punishment that awaited them in the hereafter (Dimont, 1962).

The Immigrant Experience

Prior to the Immigration Quota Act of 1924, immigration was an essential source of labor for the economic development of the United States. Until the early part of the nineteenth century, important numbers of European immigrants continued to come from England, France, and Germany. These were mostly farmers and artisans who brought their marketable skills and capital in order to seize upon more attractive opportunities in the New World.

But the nature of immigration changed considerably after 1840, when sizable groups of landless peasants from Ireland and Germany arrived in the United States. Lacking either resources or skills, most of these immigrants had only their labor to sell and therefore managed to secure a marginal existence for themselves and their families. The distribution of immigrants by area of the United States was directly related to the presence of opportunities for unskilled labor.

Immigration from Ireland and Germany persisted at a respectable level beyond the turn of the twentieth century at the same time that new sources of immigration began to mount in importance. After 1870, economic problems in Scandinavia brought a large and growing number of Scandinavians to the shores of America. And only a decade later, the same social and economic changes in Eastern and Southern Europe resulted in an increasing volume of emigration to the United States and elsewhere. Between 1880 and World War I, large numbers of

Italians and Eastern European Jews entered the United States. Smaller groups of newcomers also arrived from Greece and Rumania, and from the Slavic and Baltic nations. Like those before them, the members of these immigrant groups were predominately peasants without skills or money who were forced to enter the lowest levels of the American labor market.

Upon their arrival, these immigrants were faced with the unenviable task of getting work immediately in order to sustain their lives. They had little choice since they desperately needed jobs and could not afford to negotiate wages, hours, or working conditions. As a result, many immigrants were exploited by employers who found a willing labor pool for poor pay and miserable working conditions. What is more, a growing prejudice against these newcomers often developed to justify their continued exploitation, keeping them tied to lowly positions in the economic order (Handlin, 1962).

The impact of immigration on America's expanding industrialism cannot easily be exaggerated:

> Without the immigrants America could not have found quickly enough the manpower to build the railroads, mine the coal, man the open-hearth steel furnaces, and run the machines. Moreover, while most of the immigrants were pushed into the unskilled, backbreaking jobs, enough of them were skilled— carrying over techniques from a European industrialism which had made an earlier start—so that the Great Migration was not only one of people but of talents, skills, and cultural traditions. [Lerner, 1972:114.]

The Impact of Slavery

Slavery in the antebellum South gives more brutal but decisive testimony of the economic importance of prejudice, a factor that permitted justifying the enslavement of millions of human beings in order to provide cheap labor for an expanding agricultural economy. The American version of slavery may have derived its initial impetus from an acute labor shortage existing in Colonial America that could not be resolved adequately by means of European manpower. At least half of the white European immigrants to Colonial America paid their passage to the New World by obligating themselves as servants for periods of from two to seven years (Stampp, 1956). When sources of white labor threatened to dry up, however, America shifted its attention to Africa:

> The master could not sustain white servitude without risking the eventual cutoff of Europeans coming to the New World. But with no such possibility existing with respect to Africans, since few blacks were voluntarily entering the colonies anyway, the color line soon developed into a conspicuous, distinguishing feature between free and slave labor. Through this course, according to Oscar Handlin, the inferiority associated with servitude transferred to the color black; virtual lifetime bondage became the lot only of Negroes. The arrangement, moreover, provided an economic incentive for aggressive recruitment of slaves from the black continent.* [Wilhelm, 1970:127.]

Southerners could have turned entirely to free white labor, but they would have sacrificed the several advantages that only slavery could have provided. In the first place, an average white laborer was paid more than the cost of investing in and maintaining his enslaved counterpart. Second, the slave owner was far better able to exploit black women and children. Third, a

---

* For a period of time, American Indians also were enslaved by the white colonials. However, several factors determined that the general trend of policy toward American Indians would be against their enslavement. First, their adaptation to plantation life was impeded by cultural factors. Second, Indians could often escape to the protection of their own tribes located in proximity to the plantation. Third, early white settlers feared neighboring Indians and sought their friendship more than their labor. As a result, a predominantly Negro ancestry became the requirement for enslavement (Stampp, 1956).

master could require his slaves to work longer hours under more difficult conditions without having to negotiate with his workers or with their organizations. Finally, slave ownership was a symbol of status that identified the master with a privileged social class in the South (Stampp, 1956).*

In the Southern colonies, a few powerful persons, predominantly planters, shared a need for numerous slaves who could be trained and controlled for profitable exploitation (Noel, 1968). As a result, the vast majority of Southern slaves filled the roles of field hands and domestic servants, though smaller numbers of slaves were employed as needed in saltworks, mines, railroad construction, textile mills, and in other occupations that required specialized skills (Logan, 1954). Also as a result of the need for exploitable labor, slavery soon came to be regarded as a kind of "white man's burden," as a moral and religious obligation on the part of white Southerners that was divinely ordained and ultimately beneficial to the "uncivilized" and "inferior" black slave (Comer, 1972; Genovese, 1969).

Contemporary American Society

The economic exploitation of black Americans continued long after the resolution of the Civil War. The continued presence of institutionalized forms of prejudice against blacks assured that many Southern whites would go on avoiding the dirty work of their communities—work requiring heavy manual labor or the performance of monotonous tasks and paying low wages (Dollard, 1938).

The same phenomenon has been observed to occur in other parts of the United States, where the nature of the minority

* Though slavery benefited a small group of masters, the economic profitability of slave labor for the South as a whole is a debatable issue that involves the relative advantages and disadvantages of one-crop agriculture, soil exhaustion, and long-run differences between agriculture and manufacturing, to mention only a few of the relevant issues.

selected to perform unpleasant or low-paying jobs is determined by the historical presence of its members in the population of that area. For example, the economy of eastern Oklahoma depends on its sizable population of Cherokee Indians to provide an inexpensive and permanent labor supply for the low-paying manual work of the region. In the 1960s, Cherokee median per capita income was approximately $500. "In some areas, Cherokees live in virtual peonage; in others, straw bosses recruit Cherokee laborers for irregular work at low pay" (Wahrhaftig and Thomas, 1969:195).

The changing character of California's farm workers similarly illustrates the influence of sheer availability on the fate of minority Americans. California Indians were the state's first farm workers, coming on the scene at a time when agricultural production was essentially limited to cattle and wheat. But a subsequent influx of Chinese immigrants soon changed the nature of farm work in California. By 1870, as work on the transcontinental railroad was coming to an end, Chinese laborers turned for work to California's farmlands. The availability of this large supply of Chinese labor was an important factor in the shift in California's agricultural patterns from livestock and wheat to fruits and vegetables, crops which required larger amounts of hand labor.

The supply of Chinese labor for California agriculture was sharply reduced when, in 1882, Congress suspended Chinese immigration. Shortly thereafter, however the Japanese government decided to lift its ban on emigration and sizable numbers of workers from the rice paddies of Japan began to appear in California. Until the early decades of the twentieth century, when anti-Japanese prejudice appeared in full force, the Japanese were a major source of farm labor in California. After 1910, however, the turmoil of a revolution in Mexico persuaded tens of thousands of rural Mexicans to flee to the safety and security of the United States. From that time to the present day, Mexicans have continued to represent the most important

"Ability grouping" is a method of educational tracking whereby students are sorted into homogeneous groups on the basis of "their ability to perform classroom tasks" such as reading or arithmetic. With respect to higher education, ability grouping may determine whether or not a child can enter college or, if he does extend his education, whether or not he is able to attend a prestige school. Howe and Lauter (1972) argue that ability grouping helps to ensure that low-paying and unpleasant occupations are supplied with manpower while white, middle-class children are being prepared to fill the technological and professional needs of our society. In the following excerpt from "How the School System Is Rigged for Failure," Howe and Lauter present evidence for their view:

> Ability grouping has been operating effectively to limit competition with the children of white, middle-class parents who, on the whole, have controlled the schools. In New York City in 1967, for example, nonwhites, the vast majority of them poor, made up 40 percent of the high school population; they constituted about 36 percent of students in the "academic" high schools and about 60 percent of those tracked into "vocational" high schools. In the Bronx High School of Science and in Brooklyn Tech, elite institutions for which students must qualify by examination, "nonwhites" totaled only 7 and 12 percent of the students respectively.

> But the real effects of tracking can better be seen in the statistics of students in the academic high schools. A majority of blacks and Puerto Ricans fill lower tracks, which lead them—if they stay at all—to "general" rather than "academic" diplomas. Only 18 percent of academic high school graduates were black or Puerto Rican (though they were, as we said, 36 percent of the academic student population); and only one-fifth of that 19 percent went on to college, as compared with 63 percent of whites who graduated. In other words, only 7 percent of the graduates of New York's academic high schools who went on to college were black or Puerto Rican. The rest, for the most part tracked into non-college-preparatory programs, left school with what amounted to a ticket into the Army. [1972: 232–233.]

source of farm labor in California (London and Anderson, 1970).

Present-day attitudes and norms regarding minority Americans still reflect the existence of a need to fill low-paying and unpleasant jobs: As Glenn's (1966) data indicate, black subordination in the 1960s helped to reduce the cost of labor to employers, especially in the South. The presence of large numbers of blacks in the population of a locality increased the availability of domestic help to Southern white housewives and helped to reduce the cost of operatives and laborers to many Southern employers.

Despite popular beliefs to the contrary, prejudice against black Americans actually may help to *lower* the wages of certain white as well as black workers, while providing higher incomes for more affluent whites. Reich (1972) examined this possibility by studying the income distributions found in the forty-eight largest metropolitan areas of the United States. Using data from the 1960 census, Reich determined that in areas where black median family income was low relative to white median family income there was also greater income inequality *among* whites. More specifically, relatively low black income in an area was associated with increased income for wealthy white families and with decreased income for middle-income white families.* According to Reich, a number of mechanisms explain this relationship. In the first place, divisions between black and white workers inhibit the development

---

* Differences between the analyses of Reich (1972) and Glenn (1963) should be noted. First of all, Reich focused upon low black income as an indicator of racism, whereas Glenn was concerned with the relative frequency of blacks in a given population as related to the occupational status of whites. Moreover, Glenn examined the effect of the presence of a large black population on occupational advantages for whites *overall*, whereas Reich focused directly on *inequality* among whites. It is, of course, conceivable that both overall occupational status of whites as well as inequalities among them tend to increase as a result of either the relative frequency of blacks or of black income.

of united worker organizations that could effectively represent the demands of labor. For instance, the barring of blacks from white labor unions has resulted in the use of blacks as strikebreakers—an arrangement from which employers have benefited (Meier and Rudwick, 1966). Secondly, racial antagonisms prevent whites and blacks from joining in a united political movement in order to secure improved educational opportunities for their children. Finally, the "relative satisfaction" that results from comparing their educational opportunities against the inferior opportunities available to blacks may reduce the desire of some whites to take political action for improved schools.

MAINTENANCE OF POWER

The power leadership of a society may owe part of its capacity for survival to the presence of institutionalized forms of prejudice against minority groups. Throughout history, various minorities have been selected by the majority group as "servants of power."

Court Jews and Renegade Christians

The position of Jews in seventeenth- and eighteenth-century Germany provides a case in point. The Jews held only a marginal position in the social structure of the larger German society, having no citizen rights or legal protections and being widely despised and persecuted by the German people. As a result, German Jews, taken from the squalor of the ghetto, found themselves at the mercy of the Germanic absolutist rulers who utilized them as instruments for maximizing their power in society. As servants of power to these rulers, court Jews became advisors, collaborators, bankers, and financiers:

> Jewish financiers and entrepreneurs supplied the armies of
> their prince, financed his wars, arranged new loans and settled
> old debts. They supplied the jewels for the prince's wife and
> his mistresses, but they also were innovators in building up
> trade and industry in defiance of guild restrictions. At times
> they monopolized the trade in silver, salt, or tobacco. They
> built silk, ribbon, cloth, and velvet factories in Prussia; they
> were chief tax collectors and diplomatic representatives,
> financial administrators and bankers, but above all confidants
> of the prince. [Coser, 1972:578.]

As Coser (1972) points out, renegade Christians were
similarly employed by fourteenth- and fifteenth-century Turkish
sultans who sought to maintain and extend their power over
their Muslim subjects. Taken as youth and converted to the
Muslim faith, these nonnative Christians became important
human resources for the sultan's staff, serving in both civilian
and military capacities as courtiers, administrators, and military
officers. Renegade Christians provided Turkish rulers with a
loyal and ambitious staff. Being the slaves of a single ruler as
well as outsiders from the standpoint of the native population,
they were totally dependent upon the sultan, who, in turn,
became freed from reliance on the support of his native Muslim
population.

The Safety-Valve Function

The consequences of prejudice for maintaining power are sometimes directly visible to the members of a society; other times,
however, such consequences take indirect and subtle forms that
are dependent on the operation and interplay of both psychological as well as sociological mechanisms. As shown in Chapter
2, the tendency to find a scapegoat, or displace aggression, may
become incorporated into the personality dynamics of an
individual, often providing for the immediate gratification of his
irrational ego-defensive needs and desires. Among highly preju-

diced persons, there seems to be an extreme unwillingness to attribute blame to the dominant sources of power in society. In an effort to compensate for feelings of weakness and inferiority, prejudiced individuals instead seek to identify themselves with powerful persons and groups, typically attributing their frustrations to members of minority groups (Berkowitz, 1962).

On a collective level, scapegoating may serve as a *safety valve* whereby feelings of hostility are diverted to substitute objects, thereby protecting the leaders of a group from becoming the recipients of aggression (Coser 1956). This phenomenon has been observed in the confines of the small-group laboratory.

Burke (1969) has shown, for example, that the displacement of hostility upon a low-status member of a small group can become a mechanism whereby the task leader escapes the hostility of other group members.

Outside of the experimental laboratory, the safety-valve function of scapegoating often protects powerful persons in a society from the unmitigated hostility of its members. According to Sherman, at least part of this function is carried out by dividing the members of society along majority-minority lines, so that interests shared by both groups become obscured and hostility is directed downward in the system of social class, rather than toward a common opponent located at the top:

> For example, no one is more oppressed or poverty-stricken than the white sharecropper of the South (except the black sharecropper). But he has always fought against his natural allies, and supported the wealthy white Southerners to the extent that they not only monopolize Southern politics but achieve the chairmanship of most congressional committees by seniority. Similarly, the white worker is set against the black worker, so that unionization is prevented altogether in many Southern areas, and each can be used as a strikebreaker against the other. The same kind of divide and rule tactic is used in Northern cities. [1972:180–181.]

McWilliams (1948) has argued that the anti-Semitism that emerged in full force during the closing decades of nineteenth-century America originated in significant part with wealthy industrial tycoons who utilized prejudice as a tactic for diverting attention from their greedy labor practices and for maintaining power and wealth. Under the active encouragement of these tycoons, anti-Semitism became a "mask for privilege" that quickly spread in scope to encompass wider and wider sectors of American society.

Rigid social structures such as totalitarian societies seem to be especially dependent for their existence on the safety-valve function of scapegoating (Coser, 1956). The institutionalization of anti-Semitism in Nazi Germany provides an appropriate example: The Jews were widely viewed by the members of German society as being directly responsible for the severe economic problems that plagued them. In an experimental context, Lippitt and White (1958) similarly report that children who participated in an autocratic group atmosphere tended to express their hostility against one of the children in their group or against members of outgroups rather than against the authoritarian leader.

SUMMARY AND CONCLUSION

In this chapter, we have examined the social functions of prejudice for the majority group—those consequences of a political or economic nature that help the majority group to maintain its advantaged position in a society. The emphasis has been on intergroup conflict. As Weber (Gerth and Mills, 1946) long ago suggested, the structured inequalities of a society may involve differences between individuals with respect to the dimensions of status, economic resources, and power. Thus, the present chapter has focused on the consequences of prejudice for (1) the maintenance of occupational status, (2) the performance of unpleasant or low-paying jobs, and (3) the maintenance of power.

When the maintenance of the status of the majority group depends on the continued subordination of a minority, then intergroup competition tends to be translated into prejudice. Indeed, many of the most visible benefits of prejudice for the majority group have a rational economic basis, occurring as the minority-group member seeks to secure a share of the scarce resources of his society. This has been true historically for many of the minorities in America including Germans, Chinese, and blacks. For Mexican-Americans and American Indians, prejudice against them has been associated with organized efforts on the part of white Americans to secure land and extend political boundaries.

There is evidence to suggest that the relationship between minority-group subordination and majority-group occupational status applies to contemporary American society as well. For example, localities with large black populations have more favorable occupational status among whites. Moreover, anti-black sentiment in our society continues to be most pronounced among those individuals who are most anxious to protect their small amounts of power and status.

The flip side of the economic function of prejudice must be given its due emphasis. Prejudice justifies placing members of the minority in a position to serve the majority group, whether by taking low-paying jobs or by performing important tasks which the majority does not itself elect to perform.

Examples of the importance of this function can be found throughout history. During the Middle Ages, European Jews were generally restricted to the despised but essential occupation of lending money at interest. Immigrant labor was essential to a rapidly expanding American industrialism. In the antebellum South, millions of human beings were enslaved in order to provide cheap labor for an expanding agricultural economy. As a contemporary example, the presence of large numbers of blacks in a locality ensures that domestic help will be available to white housewives and helps to reduce the cost of laborers to white employers. The historical presence of such minorities as Chinese, Japanese, and Mexicans has influenced the character of California agriculture.

The power leadership of a society may owe part of its capacity for survival to the presence of prejudice against minorities. Throughout history, various minority groups have been chosen as "servants of power." The position of Jews in seventeenth- and eighteenth-century Germany provides a case in point. Certain German Jews became advisors, collaborators, bankers, and financiers to Germanic absolutist rulers. In a similar way, renegade Christians were employed by fourteenth- and fifteenth-century Turkish sultans who sought to maintain and extend their power over their Muslim subjects.

The consequences of prejudice for maintaining power may take more indirect and subtle forms. On a collective level, scapegoating may serve as a *safety valve* whereby feelings of hostility are diverted to substitute objects, thereby protecting the leaders of a group from becoming the recipients of aggression. At least part of this function is carried out by dividing the members of society along majority-minority lines, so that interests shared by both groups become obscured and hostility is directed downward in the system of social class, rather than toward a common opponent located at the top.

Up to this point, we have examined the consequences of prejudice for majority-group members. In the following chapter, we turn our attention to the functions of prejudice for the minority group, the very individuals against whom hostility has been directed.

chapter four
FUNCTIONS OF PREJUDICE FOR THE MINORITY GROUP

The functions of prejudice frequently manifest themselves as positive consequences for the members of a majority group either at the personality level or at the level of group maintenance. From this standpoint, elements within the majority group clearly represent the major obstacle to progress toward full equality for a minority group. Subordination could not be sustained for any length of time or with any effectiveness if it were not for the presence of important majority-group interests and needs that are being served (or are perceived as being served) by the maintenance of prejudice.

Having examined the range of such functions for the majority group, we turn our attention now to the consequences of prejudice for minority-group members, the very persons against whom the hostility of the majority group has been directed. What are the secondary gains and special opportunities that exist in a minority group by virtue of the hostility that confronts it? How do certain members of a minority group come to "take advantage of the disadvantages" that have been imposed upon them? The implications of this inquiry for our purposes are clear: To the extent that such minority-group functions of prejudice actually occur, there may be certain resistances to total equality located within the minority group itself, resistances that operate to reinforce and support the interests of the majority group and that must be identified and overcome in order to reduce the level of prejudice in a society. The present chapter has been organized around the following consequences for the minority group: (1) the reduction of competition, (2) the maintenance of solidarity, and (3) the reduction of uncertainty.

REDUCTION OF COMPETITION

To acknowledge the presence in a minority group of opposition to equality is to recognize that prejudice can transcend lines of ethnicity and link itself to interests apart from those of race, religion, or national origin. For Rose (1951), the willingness of minority-group members to turn to personal advantage the prejudice directed against them may indicate the presence of group self-hatred. This occurs when personal desires for political or economic gain conflict with the needs and interests of the group as a whole.

Frazier recognized the presence of such economic and political gains among certain black Americans, when he wrote about "the Negro's vested interest in segregation." According to Frazier, it was primarily the middle-class black—the business-man, teacher, social worker, physician, and clergyman—who benefited from the impact of segregation and discrimination, for it was he who enjoyed the advantage of being guarded from competing with his white occupational counterpart. Preferring the security achieved by a monopoly of occupations within the segregated black community, certain black professionals and businessmen adopted ambivalent attitudes toward the possibility of integration and created rationalizations about the peculiar needs of black Americans or about prejudice against blacks in nonsegregated occupational settings:

> Thus, Negro physicians may advocate separate hospitals on the grounds that in them they would have more opportunities to develop their skill and to serve their "own people." But this, too, is only a rationalization because there is abundant evidence that the standard of medical care in segregated hospitals, where Negro physicians are supposed to have every professional opportunity, is lower than in unsegregated institutions. It is scarcely necessary to point out that to abolish segregation would create technological unemployment for Negroes who secure a living from the existence of segregation. [1951:335.]

How accurate were Frazier's observations regarding the attitudes of some black professionals? Are such individuals actually hesitant to compete with their white counterparts? In order to shed light on these and related questions, Howard interviewed a sample of a hundred black male physicians, dentists, lawyers, and teachers regarding their attitudes toward competition with whites. These were the very individuals who might have had some interest in maintaining the relatively closed system of competition that accompanies prejudice and segregation against blacks, since it provides them with a virtual monopoly of services to other blacks.

Howard's respondents were asked to indicate their agreement or disagreement with a series of items including hypothetical situations such as the following:

Dr. J, who is a white physician, opened an office in an all-Negro neighborhood about 6 months ago. Recently, he advised a white physician friend to open an office in the same neighborhood. The white friend decided to open the office. Negro physicians in the neighborhood heard about the decision of Dr J's friend and urged him not to open the office. They advised him on several desirable locations in all-white neighborhoods. How do you feel about the advice of the Negro physicians? [1966:23.]

Howard's findings lend support to the observations made earlier by Frazier: These black professionals were less than enthusiastic about the notion of intergroup competition; their general position being only *slightly* in agreement with open competition with whites. This ambivalence of black professionals toward open competition applied across the board to the members of all four sample groups—physicians, dentists, lawyers, and teachers.

Howard refers to the source of ambivalence among black professionals as the "Negro dilemma"; their commitment to the democratic goal of free competition prevented them from becoming strongly opposed to competition with whites; yet their economic and social interests in segregation inhibited the development of very favorable attitudes toward such competition.

MAINTENANCE OF SOLIDARITY

In the nineteenth century, Simmel (1955) suggested that an external threat could reduce the tensions and strengthen the solidarity within a group. An everyday example of this phenomenon is provided by Sherif's study of the production of intergroup conflict among eleven-year-old campers. Competition and conflict between the two groups of boys resulted in "renewed efforts at in-group coordination, planning new tactics or engaging in acts directed against the out-group, and the like . . ." (1956:311). The common purpose supplied by intergroup friction quickly submerged internal discord, so that negative feelings and beliefs could be focused on the members of the rival group.

Intergroup conflict has long been thought to contribute to group cohesiveness in many contexts:

> The confrontation between police and protesters in Chicago had a divisive effect on the community and the society, but it solidified group feeling within the police department and also served to unify the protesting factions. A religious sect that breaks away from an established Church to initiate some type of reform is likely to become increasingly close-knit as conflict develops with the larger group. A society fighting for its very existence against a common enemy, as Great Britain did during World War II, often exhibits a powerful sense of determination and will to resist as individuals subordinate their personal interests to the welfare of their country. [DeFleur, D'Antonio, and DeFleur, 1971:58.]

In a similar way, it can be said that the internal cohesion of a minority group is frequently enhanced as a result of an external threat to it. It would appear, for instance, that anti-Semitism has had a profound influence on the internal solidarity of the Jews, frequently isolating them from the non-Jewish population and strengthening their determination to preserve their religious identity. This is the phenomenon that Theodor Herzl had in mind when he asserted, "We are a people—the enemy makes us a people."

From the standpoint of some observers, the Jews would

Group solidarity frequently takes the form of ingroup pride and hostility toward members of the majority group. Harry Golden's account of his early impressions of Christians provides an interesting illustration:

> My first impressions of Christianity came in the home, of course. My parents brought with them the burden of the Middle Ages from the blood-soaked continent of Europe. They had come from the villages of Eastern Europe where Christians were feared with legitimate reason.

> When occasionally a Jewish drunk was seen in our neighborhood, our parents would say, "He's behaving like a Gentile."

> For in truth, our parents had often witnessed the Polish, Romanian, Hungarian, and Russian peasants gather around a barrel of whiskey on Saturday night, drink themselves into oblivion, "and beat their wives." Once in a while the rumor would spread through the tenements that a fellow had struck his wife, and on all sides we heard the inevitable, "Just like a Gentile."

> Oddly enough, too, our parents had us convinced that the Gentiles were noisy, boisterous, and loud—unlike the Jews. It is indeed strange how often stereotypes are exactly reversed.

> If we raised our voices, we were told, "Jewish boys don't shout." And this admonition covered every activity in and out of the home: "Jewish boys don't fight." "Jewish boys don't get dirty." "Jewish boys study hard."

> It wasn't until I was in school and was subjected to the influence of Gentile teachers and met Gentile social workers and classmates that I began to question these generalizations. Then I began to read and I found myself finally dismissing all prejudice from my mind. I still had a vague idea that the Jews were *very* special with God, but I discarded the notion that He was disinterested in or hostile to the Gentiles. [1962:210.]

probably not have maintained themselves as Jews historically
without the continued presence of considerable hostility from
the Christian world (van den Haag, 1969). It may also be the
case that the rapid rate of Jewish upward mobility in the United
States can be regarded, at least in some part, as a defensive
reaction to anti-Semitism. More specifically, it may be seen as
a compensatory mechanism whereby economic achievement is
assigned a high value by Jewish Americans who seek to escape
their socioeconomically and culturally marginal position in society. In a similar way, the relative success of Japanese Americans in regard to their quest for increased socioeconomic status
may have been aided by the presence of the same hostility which
was often used against them by white Americans (Caudill and
Vos, 1966).

The cohesiveness of a minority may decline as an external
threat to the group decreases. Thus, Jews in America continue
to participate rather extensively in activities related to the survival of Judaism (Lazarwitz, 1970), whereas Israeli Jews may
be losing their Jewish identity in favor of an association with the
State of Israel. The transference of ethnic identity from Judaism
to Zionism seems to reflect the impact of a perceived and actual
threat to the persistence of the Jewish State from its hostile
neighbors (Hofman, 1970) as well as the unique presence of a
Jewish majority group in Israeli society that no longer confronts
hardship, hostility, or hatred based on its *religious* identity.

As seen, prejudice directed against a minority group often
exerts pressure for group cohesiveness and pride, forces emphasis on its history and achievements, and brings about the
development of organizations which further its interests. Yet
external threat may sometimes diminish rather than heighten
the morale of group members. For instance, if a minority group
has previously experienced severe deprivation of group identity,
the external pressure of prejudice from the majority group
tends to demoralize its members and heighten intragroup con-

Group-unifying elements of "black power" have been represented in the following statement by Stokely Carmichael and Charles V. Hamilton:

> Black people must redefine themsleves, and only *they*
> can do that. Throughout this country, vast segments of the
> black communities are beginning to recognize the need
> to assert their own definitions, to reclaim their history,
> their culture; to create their own sense of community and
> togetherness. There is a growing resentment of the word
> "Negro," for example, because this term is the invention
> of our oppressor; it is *his* image of us that he describes.
> Many blacks are now calling themselves African-Americans, Afro-Americans or black people because that is *our*
> image of ourselves. When we begin to define our own
> image, the stereotypes—that is, lies—that our oppressor
> has developed will begin in the white community and end
> there. The black community will have a positive image of
> itself that *it* has created. This means we will no longer call
> ourselves lazy, apathetic, dumb, good-timers, shiftless, etc.
> Those are words used by white America to define us. If
> we accept these adjectives, as some of us have in the past,
> then we see ourselves only in a negative way, precisely the
> way white America wants us to see ourselves. Our incentive
> is broken and our will to fight is surrendered. From now
> on we shall view ourselves as African-Americans and as
> black people who are in fact energetic, determined, intelligent, beautiful and peace-loving. [1967:37–38.]

flict. Thus, in the collective experience of black America, prejudice has contributed to a diminution of group solidarity, leading to rejection and escape more than to any sense of group spirit. It was not until the expectations of black Americans had risen sufficiently that group solidarity could be regarded as a widespread response to anti-black prejudice (Yinger, 1961). In the recent experiences of black America, group solidarity and pride have been an important dimension of the broader phenomenon of "black power," in which mistrust of whites, racial separation, black capitalism, violence, and community control have played a part (MacDonald, 1971).

REDUCTION OF UNCERTAINTY

Just as it operates to structure the world of the majority-group member, so prejudice can help to define the situation of the minority-group member who seeks to create a degree of psychological security out of an otherwise unfriendly, if not threatening, social environment. Given the nature of such conditions in society, it is not surprising that, as a well-known journalist has recently asserted, "segregation is an affliction, but for many it is a crutch as well" (Silberman, 1964:11).

The role expectations and prescriptions for subordinated groups in a society represent the burden of oppression for those individuals who must fulfill them. But all expectations and prescriptions also lend a psychologically comfortable level of predictability to the social relationships in which such individuals are involved, in some cases producing a kind of "social inertia," a compromise between the desire for equality of opportunity, on the one hand, and the need for certainty, on the other.

Many individuals may have a desire to achieve a *defined status* within a group; they may actively seek to arrive at a clear-cut social position for themselves, whether it be defined as high or low in the eyes of others (Prosterman, 1972). Viewed in this way, it becomes easier to understand why Helen Lynch (1972), a woman writing for a large Boston newspaper, would declare that "equality would be a demotion." For this columnist, "equal status with the men in my life" would be an undesirable end!

An important consequence of prejudice in its capacity to reduce uncertainty is to locate the source of problems experienced by a minority-group member in the social system rather than in his own inadequacy. In this regard, Cloward and Ohlin have argued that "when external barriers to the achievement of success-goals and their influence on the criteria of evaluation are clearly apparent, it is much more likely that persons who fail to achieve their aspirations will attribute failure to the social order rather than to themselves" (1960:121).

In the context of black-white relations, the availability of a system-blame explanation of personal shortcomings that clearly has a good deal of validity may keep many blacks from suffering a great loss of self-esteem. For individuals who locate the source of their problems in personal inadequacy, failure results in low self-regard. By contrast, individuals who ascribe their failure to the system tend to withdraw their loyalty from the system and attack it in either a direct or indirect manner (McCarthy and Yancey, 1971). It is significant to note that, despite the well-known sociological truism that blacks suffer from low self-esteem, recent evidence instead suggests that black Americans do not have lower self-esteem, and may even have higher self-esteem, than whites (Heiss and Owens, 1972; Yancey, Rigsby and McCarthy, 1972). In support of this contention, Parker and Kleiner (1968) have shown that mental illness tends to be less severe among those blacks who perceive "being a Negro" as a barrier to achievement. Moreover, the relatively low suicide rate among black Americans may indicate the presence of "external restraints" in the form of a well-defined set of expectations from which blacks have lacked the freedom to deviate (Henry and Short, 1954).

SUMMARY AND CONCLUSION

Opposition to full equality for American minorities can be located for the largest part in elements of the majority group that perceive their interests or needs as depending upon the continuance of prejudice against the members of a minority. So far-reaching is the prejudice of the majority, however, that it often overlaps the boundaries that separate majority from minority. In such circumstances, certain elements of a minority may identify their interests or needs with the maintenance of the status quo and come to resist the idea of full equality for the members of their own group.

We emphasize once again that the resistances within the minority group are minimal and secondary when compared with those found within the majority which, by definition, has greater capacity to realize its will. We stress also that the minority group contains within it major forces for the breakdown of prejudiced attitudes and institutions. Clearly, for example, many individuals and groups within the black community have provided the major thrust of important civil rights activities over the last few decades, activities that could lead to significant progress toward achieving equality.

On the whole, prejudice has been culturally, if not physically, debilitating in its consequences for minority groups. Yet we must also recognize the presence of vested interests and special opportunities among certain elements of minority groups specifically having to do with the reduction of competition, the maintenance of solidarity, and the reduction of uncertainty— secondary gains that remain dependent upon the continuance of prejudice against members of the minority group.

To acknowledge the presence in a minority group of opposition to equality is to recognize that prejudice can transcend lines of ethnicity and link itself to interests apart from those of race, religion, or national origin. Such economic and political gains may occur among certain black Americans; namely middle-class black businessmen, teachers, social workers, physicians, and clergymen, who have been guarded from competition with their white occupational counterparts. As a result, such black professionals and businessmen may adopt ambivalent attitudes toward the possibility of integration, and create rationalizations about the peculiar needs of blacks in America.

The consequences of prejudice for the minority group can be less deliberate. In the nineteenth century, Simmel suggested that an external threat could reduce the tensions and strengthen the solidarity within a group. It would appear that anti-Semitism has had a profound influence on the internal solidarity of the Jews, frequently isolating them from the non-Jewish population and strengthening their determination to preserve their religious identity.

Prejudice directed against a minority group often exerts pressure for group cohesiveness and pride, forces emphasis on its history and achievement, and brings about the development of organizations which further its interests as a group. Yet external threat may also have the opposite effect, especially in a minority group that has experienced severe deprivation and loss of group identity. Thus, in the collective experience of black America, prejudice has contributed to a diminution of group solidarity, leading to escape and retreat more than to any sense of group spirit. It was not until the expectations of black Americans had risen sufficiently that group solidarity could be regarded as a widespread response to anti-black prejudice.

Just as it operates to structure the world of the majority-group member, so prejudice can help to define the situation of the minority-group member who seeks to create a degree of psychological security out of an otherwise unfriendly, if not threatening, social environment. An important consequence of prejudice in its capacity to reduce uncertainty is to locate the source of problems experienced by a minority-group member in the social system rather than in his own inadequacy. In the context of black-white relations, the availability of a system-blame explanation of personal shortcomings that *clearly has a good deal of validity* may keep many blacks from suffering a great loss of self-esteem.

In the final chapter, we focus our attention on the nature, or essential characteristics, of American society. Using a functional framework, we attempt to identify possible determinants of prejudice and to link them to the consequences discussed in previous chapters.

chapter five

PREJUDICE IN AMERICAN SOCIETY

Scholars focusing upon the dysfunctional consequences of prejudice have rightly drawn the attention of social science as well as society to the costly and morally unacceptable impact of prejudice. But they have done little to explain the tenacious hold of prejudice on the members of our society or to provide meaningful suggestions for its reduction.

As we have seen, prejudice can be treated as an *independent variable,* a causal factor that has certain consequences for society and its members. From a broader perspective, however, prejudice also acts as an *intervening variable* between important psychological and sociocultural forces, on the one hand, and individual responses, on the other, or between the factors responsible for the maintenance of prejudice and the functions that prejudice performs. Specifically, our focus has been upon such causal factors as (1) frustration-aggression, (2) threat to self-esteem, (3) the need to reduce uncertainty, and (4) competition for power, status, and wealth.

We now ask, what are the sociocultural characteristics that

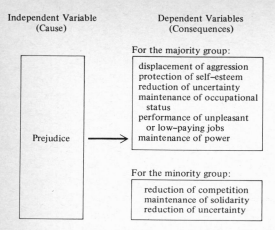

Figure 5–1.   Prejudice as an independent variable

interact with, support, or underlie such causal factors as frustration, threat to self-esteem, uncertainty, and competition. What factors make it possible for prejudice to persist in our society? What is it about the character of our society that helps to sustain the functional nature of prejudice? In this regard, we

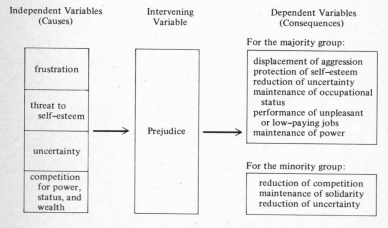

Figure 5–2.   Prejudice as an intervening variable

choose to stress the operation in our society of *competitiveness* and *rapid social change* as characteristics of particular relevance.*

COMPETITIVENESS AND PREJUDICE IN AMERICAN SOCIETY

To characterize American society as competitive may be to understate the obvious. Foreign observers have frequently noted the admiration of Americans for competitive effort and for the acquisition of wealth (Torrence and Meadows, 1958). Social scientists have similarly concluded that American society emphasizes competitive success and the competitive grading of its members (Williams, 1965). Horney described American social relationships in the following way:

> The isolated individual has to fight with other individuals of the same group, has to surpass them and, frequently, thrust them aside. The advantage of the one is frequently the disadvantage of the other . . . competitiveness, and the potential hostility that accompanies it, pervades all human relationships. . . . It pervades the relationships between men and men, between women and women, and whether the point of competition be popularity, competence, attractiveness or any other social value it greatly impairs the possibilities of reliable friendship. [1937:285–286.]

* We should stress that neither characteristic is regarded as a *necessary* condition for prejudice, but only for its particular *functional consequences*. For instance, competitiveness may turn out to be a prerequisite for the esteem-enhancing functions of prejudice, but more or less unrelated to its capacity for reducing cognitive uncertainties. Similarly, prejudice can occur in the absence of rapid social change, even though change serves as a contributory factor in our society. It goes without saying that numerous variables contribute to the overall level of prejudice in any given social context. What deserves careful attention here is that certain contributory factors in the persistence of prejudice also act as antecedent conditions for the functions of prejudice.

The current emphasis on wealth goes hand in hand with an orientation toward competition. More than ever, money seems to be a convenient symbol of success and failure in that it fixes the individual's *relative* position in regard to his contemporaries. In particular, money can be regarded as an adult equivalent of the grades received by a schoolchild (Gorer, 1964). A relatively high income—like A's on a report card—is a visible indicator that an individual has "made it" in relation to his fellows.

It would be a mistake to regard extreme competitiveness as characteristic of all societies. Cross-cultural studies of the development of competitive behavior have been conducted with thousands of children from more than twenty subcultures including those located in the United States, Belgium, Canada, Holand, Israel, Korea, and Mexico. The findings of such studies indicate, for example, that Anglo-American children tend to be more competitive than Mexican-American children, who, in turn, tend to be more competitive than Mexican rural children (Kagan and Madsen, 1971). Also of interest is the finding that Anglo-American children engage in rivalry even though it may be irrational to do so in terms of self-interest; that is to say, Anglo-American children are willing to forfeit their own prizes if it also means depriving their competitors of rewards (Nelson and Kagan, 1972).

If our society is particularly competitive, then we might expect newcomers from a traditional, ancestral culture to become increasingly more competitive the more they are assimilated into American society. Just such a finding has been obtained regarding Chinese-American students who become more competitive as they become better incorporated into American life and as their attitudes and interaction patterns draw them closer to Anglo-Americans (Levin and Leong, 1973).

We know that competitive tendencies in a child begin at home. For instance, the findings of Minturn and Lambert

(1964) indicate that the mothers of American children are especially likely to encourage their children to direct their aggressiveness toward peers. Moreover, American mothers tend to reinforce their children *only* when they succeed; by contrast, mothers from non-competitive cultures tend to reward their children whether or not they achieve a desired result (Nelson and Kagan, 1972).

ZERO-SUM ORIENTATION AND PREJUDICE

Implicit in the foregoing concept of competitiveness is a *psychology of scarcity,* an assumption that personal gains require the losses of others. Thus, competitive persons employ a *zero-sum orientation*: They view two or more individuals or groups as striving for the same scarce goals, with the success of one automatically implying a reduced probability that others will also attain their goals (Phillips, 1969).

In a similar way, Americans hold a zero-sum orientation to moral evaluations, with the individual gaining in moral worth only to the extent that others lose in moral worth, and vice versa (Douglas, 1970). This orientation engages the individual in a competitive struggle to upgrade himself and to downgrade others. Respectability demands deviance; good requires evil. As a result, the members of our society must construct and maintain a set of negative stereotypes of minorities, deviants, criminals, and the poor, and attempt to find public methods for stigmatizing such individuals. In some cases, it may be irrele-

---

ZERO-SUM ORIENTATION

Individual A gains five units of success $+5$
Individual B loses five units of success -5
                                            $\overline{0}$

---

vant whether or not *competition* between groups actually occurs. A minority group need not be perceived as posing a threat to the resources of the majority, but merely as deviating from its important *norms and values*.

The American version of competitiveness has important implications for an understanding of the contributions that prejudice makes to the personality of the majority member, especially those contributions involving the displacement of aggression, the protection of self-esteem, and the reinforcement of personal values. The subjective position of the lower-class white provides a case in point: If he perceives blacks as having success, then the lower-class white may see himself as failing. As a result, he experiences a keen sense of relative deprivation and seeks to "keep the Negro in his place" (Phillips, 1969: 199).

But the zero-sum orientation lies not only in the eyes of the beholder, it is deeply ingrained in the institutional arrangements of our society. Therefore, the struggle for status, power, and class has an objective reality of its own that must be confronted in the decisions of everyday life, where it often occurs:

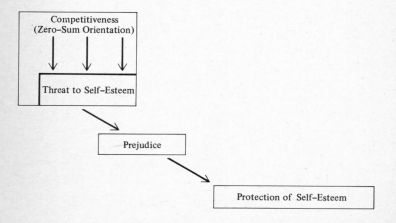

Figure 5–3. The role of prejudice in protecting self-esteem

A source of the problem is the kind of social structure where, as Horney puts it, the "advantage of the one (individual) is the disadvantage of the other." The businessman, in order to achieve his goal of success, frequently must climb over the backs of others. The basis for this kind of economic organization is the existence of scarcities in whatever it is that humans desire or value. Thus, if whatever is desired is in short supply, individuals must compete with one another for the available supply, and one man's gain is frequently another's loss.

This structuring of scarce rewards is, of course, tied in with a stratification system where there are a limited number of positions at the top relative to the large number below them. For the individual to gain the highest rewards, he must oppose the interest of others who also desire them. With such opposed interests, it becomes more difficult for the individual to interact with his competitors in cooperative ways. [Phillips, 1969:415.]

The sizable payoff for the majority group is the protection of its privileged position in our society, a position that carries a disproportionate amount of power, status, and economic means. As far as the minority is concerned, competitiveness produces many of the conditions under which prejudice creates special opportunities and advantages for certain of its members.

SOCIAL CHANGE AND PREJUDICE

Despite its importance as an explanatory variable, competitiveness does not exist in a social vacuum and should be properly regarded as but *one* of the sociocultural factors in the maintenance of prejudice. As noted by Allport (1954), rapid social change, like competitiveness, is another factor that characterizes our society and may be functionally related to the persistence of prejudice.

In relatively stable, traditional societies, it is meaningful

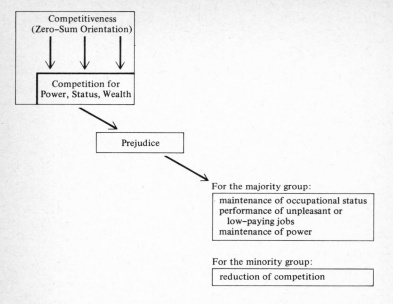

Figure 5–4.   The functions of prejudice for the majority and the
minority in the face of competitiveness

for an individual to rely upon his previous achievements as a
frame of reference for self-evaluation. Thus, a farmer might
compare his annual crop yield against the results of previous
years; a schoolchild might compare his academic performance
from one year to the next; or, the profit from a family business
might be evaluated on an annual basis.

Yet such comparisons with the past have meaning only to
the extent that structural stability can be experienced and maintained, forming a common basis for the comparison of personal
experiences. By contrast, in a rapidly changing, highly differentiated society, prior achievements provide few meaningful reference points for the present or for the future. Under the conditions
that characterize American society, standards of evaluation tend
to differ from one role to another and from one time period to

the next. Rapid change leaves its mark in the form of discontinuities between the events in our lives.

As a result, the members of American society have increasingly turned toward their contemporaries in the quest for new and more meaningful standards of evaluation. This "other-directedness" has contributed to the widespread use of relative evaluation, whereby individuals strive to outdo others around them whether at work, at school, or at play. Rapid change has created a need for *social* standards of evaluation, a need that many individuals are able to satisfy by comparing their achievements with those of their friends, classmates, or fellow employees.

In a very important sense, then, "keeping up with the Joneses" represents the presence and need for standards of evaluation as much as it represents the American brand of competitiveness. Since it contributes to relative evaluation, however, social change may help to provide conditions appropriate for the onset of zero-sum thinking which, in turn, leads to prejudice against minority-group members.

Stressful and disorienting aspects of rapid change have produced a kind of *future shock* that sweeps across the institutions of our society at an unprecedented rate. As noted by Toffler:

> . . . the final, qualitative difference between this and all previous lifetimes is the one most easily overlooked. For we have not merely extended the scope and scale of change, we have radically altered its pace. We have in our time released a totally new social force—a stream of change so accelerated that it influences our sense of time, revolutionizes the tempo of daily life, and affects the very way we "feel" the world around us. We no longer "feel" life as men did in the past. And this is the ultimate difference, the distinction that separates the truly contemporary man from all others. For this acceleration lies behind the impermanence—the transience—

THE STRESS OF ADJUSTING TO CHANGE

Events	Life-Change Units
Death of spouse	100
Divorce	73
Marital separation	65
Jail term	63
Death of close family member	63
Personal injury or illness	53
Marriage	50
Fired at work	47
Marital reconciliation	45
Retirement	45
Change in health of family member	44
Pregnancy	40
Sex difficulties	39
Gain of new family member	39
Business readjustment	39
Change in financial state	38
Death of close friend	37
Change to different line of work	36
Change in number of arguments with spouse	35
Mortgage over $10,000	31
Foreclosure of mortgage or loan	30
Change in responsibilities at work	29
Son or daughter leaving home	29
Trouble with in-laws	29
Outstanding personal achievement	28
Wife begins or stops work	26
Begin or end school	26
Change in living conditions	25
Revision of personal habits	24
Trouble with boss	23
Change in work hours or conditions	20
Change in residence	20
Change in schools	20
Change in recreation	19
Change in church activities	19
Change in social activities	18

Events	Life-Change Units
Mortgage or loan less than $10,000	17
Change in sleeping habits	16
Change in number of family get-togethers	15
Change in eating habits	15
Vacation	13
Christmas	12
Minor violations of the law	11

SOURCE: Jane E. Brody   1973   "Doctors Study Treatment of Ills Brought on by Stress." *The New York Times* (June 10):20. © 1973 by The New York Times Company. Reprinted by permission.

that penetrates and tinctures our consciousness, radically affecting the way we relate to other people, to things, to the entire universe of ideas, arts and values. [1970:17.]

If future shock actually occurs, then it must have some measurable impact on the individuals in our society. By means of a Social Readjustment Rating Scale (Holmes and Rahe, 1967), it is possible in fact to measure the adverse physiological impact of the occurrence of rapid change in an individual's life. The Scale contains forty-three life events that have been associated by means of extensive research with varying degrees of disruption in the life of the average person. Thus, "death of spouse" received 100 life-change units indicating that it requires major social readjustment, whereas "minor violations of the law" received only 11 life-change units since it generally requires minor readjustment for an individual. Using the Social Readjustment Rating Scale, it has been determined that rapid change in the individual's role—as indicated by a clustering of life events and a high life-change score—frequently precedes the onset of disease and goes to determine its severity. That is, individuals who achieve high life-change scores during a short period of time (for example, by the death of a spouse, personal injury, and retirement all in one year) are especially likely to have an illness and to experience it in a severe form (Holmes and Rahe, 1967).

But the impact of future shock extends beyond the physiological functioning of the individual. There is impressive evidence as well of the adverse psychological effects of rapid social change. For example, Mangum (1973), using a modified version of the Social Readjustment Rating Scale, has recently determined that college students who undergo rapid changes in their role relationships tend to experience greater neurotic anxiety than their counterparts who do not. High scorers on the Scale were significantly more likely to report being bothered by "trembling hands," "nightmares," "sweating," and "nervousness." Using a similar measure of the stimulation that accompanies demands of readjustment to change, Constantini, Davis, Braun, and Iervolino (1973) found that rapid change was associated with tension, depression, anger, and fatigue.

At the basis of the stress that results from rapid social change may be the individual's need for structure and his intolerance of uncertainty, whether it be of a cognitive or an emotional nature. A rapidly shifting social environment fails to provide adequate anchors for the events in an individual's life, leaving him without a sense of security or order. "On this view, the absence of a clear-cut social structure in modern societies, the presence of overlapping and confusing roles that often lead to constant changes in status position vis-à-vis various groups within which the individual moves . . . all intensely frustrate the built-in need to have a clearly defined position within the group" (Prosterman, 1972:125).

As suggested earlier, one of the consequences of prejudice for both the majority as well as the minority is to reduce cognitive and emotional uncertainties. Victims of future shock often

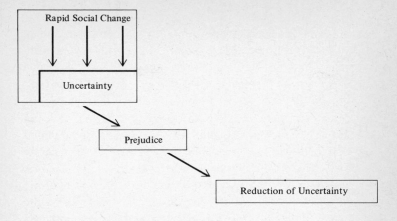

Figure 5–5. The role of prejudice in reducing uncertainty

resort to supersimplification in order to reduce the ambiguities in their environment (Toffler, 1970). They may stereotype, prejudge, find unitary solutions for the problems that confront them, all in a desperate attempt to make sense out of disorder, to structure their world in a meaningful way and to find a place for themselves in society. Durkheim (1933) referred to such a state of disorder as *anomie,* a form of social pathology in which guidelines for behavior are missing and the individual is, in a sociological sense, very much alone.

Before turning from the topic at hand, we note again that social change does not necessarily result in increased prejudice. Indeed, the historical circumstances of our own society suggest instead that a breakdown of traditional institutions has the effect of loosening the grip of prejudicial norms and attitudes. It is likely, therefore, that prejudice increases under the impact of *both* extreme stability as well as extreme change in social structure. Obviously, the content of any change must be taken into consideration as well, though the *rate* of social change can be examined in order to determine its independent influence on the level or quality of prejudice.

PROSPECTS FOR THE REDUCTION OF PREJUDICE

How do we go about reducing prejudice? On the basis of the present analysis, how can we intervene in an attempt to loosen the hold of prejudice on our society and its members? At the most fundamental societal level, we might begin by directing our efforts toward achieving a more cooperative, less competitive culture, in which a zero-sum orientation and prejudice have less meaning for an individual's self-esteem or his life-chances. Indeed, the recent decline in prejudice noted in Chapter 1 may be partially explained by the possibility that extreme competitiveness has also decreased. For example, the recent development of expressive, noncompetitive values among youth-oriented social movements such as the "beats" or the "hippies" may represent a larger process of "balancing" in American society as a whole, whereby our society, having been pushed more and more toward extreme competitiveness, is presently attempting to reduce the intensity of competitive values at all of its levels (Levin and Spates, 1970). This viewpoint has attained a good deal of popularity (Reich, 1970), though the supportive evidence is far from conclusive.

Moreover, given the extremely competitive nature of our society, it is not surprising that the acceptance of particular prejudices might rise and fall, depending upon changes in their consequences for certain groups at particular points in time. For instance, the increasing purchasing power among black Americans as sought by the producers of competing goods and services may help to determine which barriers to equality will be lifted for the members of this minority (Lerner, 1957).

At the level of major institutional change, we suggest locating an institution in American society that presently serves as a focal point for the socialization of competitiveness. Specifically, we propose to focus our attention upon the nature of formal education, a highly specialized social institution whose major function involves the transmission of the normative order from one generation to the next.

Though many investigators have studied the relationship between education and prejudice, relatively few continue to assert that formal education represents a powerful instrument for the reduction of prejudice. Selznick and Steinberg (1969) report finding an inverse relationship between anti-Semitism and amount of formal education, a relationship that could not be explained by differences in social class. Yet results claiming to demonstrate the impact of education on prejudice are extremely difficult to interpret and may demonstrate only that the educated members of our society have learned to express their prejudices publicly in subtle, more sophisticated ways, especially in the context of the paper-and-pencil questionnaires generally used by social science researchers (Stember, 1961).

In the present work, we are not concerned with the impact of the *content* of formal education as it presently exists in American society. Unlike previous approaches, we propose instead to examine the *structure* of educational programs as a potent factor in the maintenance of competitiveness.

Psychologists and sociologists have long recognized that the structure of American education depends upon social reinforcements for academic and athletic performance: Students tend to be encouraged in their efforts to exceed the achievement levels of classmates or friends. Competitiveness is emphasized, while personal improvement tends to be ignored (Coleman, 1963; Miller and Hamblin, 1963). American students come to be attracted to grading methods that can be structured toward explicit interpersonal comparisons (for example, "grading on the curve" and percentile scoring); a preference that may be an outgrowth of the essentially competitive nature of middle-class American education and, more generally, of a socialization process in which competition is regarded as a basic virtue (Turner, 1960).

To illustrate the way in which schools foster interpersonal competition, Henry relates an incident from a fifth-grade arithmetic lesson involving a student named Boris. Boris is "patiently" and "quietly" humiliated by a teacher in the presence of his classmates because he has trouble reducing a fraction to its lowest terms. After concentrating her efforts on Boris for a minute or two, the teacher then calls on another student, Peggy, who quickly offers the correct answer. The outcome is predictable:

> Boris's failure has made it possible for Peggy to succeed; his misery is the occasion for her rejoicing. This is the standard condition of the contemporary American elementary school. To a Zuñi, Hopi, or Dakota Indian, Peggy's performance would seem cruel beyond belief, for competition, the wringing of success from somebody's failure, is a form of torture foreign to those noncompetitive cultures. Yet Peggy's action seems natural to us; and so it is. How else would you run our world? [1969:205.]

The rewards given in educational contexts are capable of being structured, so that competitiveness is minimized while achievement continues to be stressed. Some recognition of the need for such a change can be found in experimental studies of the effects of interpersonal competition on group achievement and cohesion. It has been shown, for example, that competition between students in a classroom actually generates subtle but significant interference with the efforts of each student by others in the group. The result is a reduction in the overall level of achievement and in the unity of the classroom (Deutsch, 1953). As demonstrated by Deutsch, a more effective alternative to interpersonal competition among students would be to structure the learning situation in such a way that group performance can be compared with and rewarded relative to other groups. When the competition is between classrooms, each student's achievement benefits the position of other members. As a result, the students in a group support the efforts of one another. It is unfortunately true that the foregoing experiment merely substitutes one form of competition for another. Given the overwhelming presence of competitiveness, it is too often assumed that students cannot be achievement-oriented in noncompetitive educational settings. What frequently happens in the present educational structure is that individual improvement (self-evaluation) goes unrecognized and unrewarded in favor of interpersonal gain. Yet there may be a significant proportion of "noncomparers" for whom competitiveness is an alien frame of reference (Levin, 1969; Strauss, 1968). It is conceivable, as well, that a large number of students *would* be disposed to learn in a noncompetitive educational setting, if it were made available to them as an alternative. Educational psychologists are presently exploring a number of reward structures that maintain, if not heighten, achievement and have the side effect of reducing the level of competitiveness as well. Such alternatives stress the need for individualized learning, open classrooms, or student-originated objectives (Gallagher, 1970; Lerner, 1971; Neill, 1960). But they currently tend to be utilized on a limited scale in order to reach "gifted" students, children with learning disabilities, or certain children from economically advantaged homes.

An effective movement away from extreme competitiveness probably requires major institutional and individual change. At another level, however, we might still seek to develop strategies for the reduction of prejudice, without also seeking to

Failure and success in the classroom are frequently defined by students in regard to a grading mode that evaluates the achievements of any given student relative to the performance of his peers (e.g., by percentile scores) rather than relative to self-anchored performance criteria (e.g., by a student's own past performance). Children early come to have preferences for being evaluated vis-à-vis others and to direct their efforts toward the competitive struggle.

Thus, Levin and Levin (1973) hypothesized in a recent study that students who are graded with reference to the performance of other students ("you scored in the 80th percentile") would be more satisfied with their grading method than students graded with reference to their own past performance ("you got 50 percent correct on the 1st exam versus 80 percent correct on the 2nd exam"). The experimenters gave ninety-two undergraduate students a series of bogus vocabulary tests in multiple choice form that were immediately "scored by computer" and returned for the inspection of the students.

To provide a base line against which they could evaluate their subsequent test performance, all students received a grade of approximately 50 percent on the first test in the series. On the second test, half of the students were given their grades in percent form (self-comparison of grades), while half were given their grades in percentile form (social comparison of grades). Whereas the percent form permitted students to draw comparisons with their grade on the first test but not with other students, the percentile form limited their comparisons to other students who had taken the same test.

As expected, social comparison of grades (e.g., "You scored in the 80th percentile") yielded significantly greater satisfaction with the assigned grading method than self-comparison of grades (e.g., "You got 80 percent correct"). This result was obtained whether or not the student was assigned a high score on his tests. Moreover, those students who were characterized as having competitive and manipulative personality styles (Machs) were particularly oriented to the performance of their contemporaries, significantly preferring the percentile method of receiving their grades on the series of tests.

reduce competitiveness. Here, too, both psychological and sociological changes are required.

Regarding personality functions of prejudice, we might devise alternative means to maintain or enhance the self-esteem of an individual. At the present time, personal and group forms of psychotherapy—to the extent that they can increase insight and self-acceptance on the part of an individual—may provide a springboard for individualized efforts to reduce prejudice. Personal psychotherapy tends to be most effective when its overriding concern is the formation of a healthy personality. The reduction of prejudice is frequently an important by-product.

Allport relates the experience of an anti-Semitic woman who served as the respondent in a lengthy interview in depth regarding her values, attitudes, and feelings. Having reviewed her previous experiences with Jews, she finally remarked, "The poor Jews, I guess we blame them for everything, don't we? (1954:460). Her exchange with the interviewer increased her self-insight to the point where she could trace her hostility to its source and gain a new perspective on it.

Group therapy tends to be more efficient than its personal counterpart since several individuals can be simultaneously aided. Moreover, group therapy frequently operates to break down the support of prejudiced attitudes originating in the norms of the group. Haimowitz and Haimowitz (1950) provide some evidence for the influence of group therapy on the reduction of prejudice. As the individuals in their group began to feel less threatened and better able to cope with the actual source of their frustrations, they also became less hostile toward members of minority groups.

Rubin reports that sensitivity training was able to produce increased self-acceptance leading to a reduced level of prejudice. He notes that his study might just as easily have been concerned with the influence of psychotherapy upon prejudice: "Each provides the elements of psychological safety, support, and opportunities for reality testing assumed necessary to affect an increase in an individual's level of self-acceptance and consequently, by our model, decrease his level of ethnic prejudice" (1967:238).

From the standpoint of the present analysis, therapy may serve as a functional alternative to prejudice in that an individual's sense of worth can be protected or enhanced. As a significant long-term measure, however, the influence of therapy tends to be somewhat restricted. As noted earlier, therapy, even in its group form, is capable of reaching relatively few of those persons who most need it. Moreover, individuals who undergo therapy continue to be influenced, as well, by the competitive social milieu in which they live.

Any slowdown in the rate of social change might contribute to an abatement in the overall level of prejudice, but would have destructive consequences as well. Certain changes are already long overdue; others might enhance the quality of life for all members of our society. Rather than retard the rate of change, we must seek to discover the conditions under which individuals in society can best adapt themselves to change in a way that their uncertainties do not interfere with their effectiveness or psychological comfort. In this regard, Toffler (1970) notes that creative strategies are needed in order to increase the adaptivity of the individual in his reaction to change. We must experiment with tactics to regulate the level of stimulation from our social milieu and create educational or technological innovations in the socialization process to aid individuals who attempt to cope with rapid change. In this regard, Toffler suggests the development of "crisis counseling" for persons who undergo a major life change and "coping classrooms" for persons who pass through similar life transitions at the same time (e.g., prepared childbirth classes). Such tactics would provide social support for change and advance information regarding what lies ahead.

"Counteracting forces" have emerged spontaneously to offset

the adverse effects of rapid social change. Some are large-scale social movements whose common denominator may involve an ability to order the events in the lives of their adherents and reduce anomie. Witness the recent popularity of the Children of God, transcendental meditation, and the Divine Light Mission, to mention but a few. What may frequently happen in such adaptive social movements, however, is that conventional stereotypes and traditional prejudices are laid aside in favor of new forms of ingroup-outgroup, we-they distinctions. The precise impact of such movements is, at the present time, unknown.

To this point, we have been concerned with alternatives for such personality functions as the reduction of uncertainty and the protection of self-esteem. Given the ubiquitious presence of competitiveness, it is extremely difficult to suggest viable alternatives for the social functions of prejudice. It may be, as Tumin suggests, that the functional equivalents of disapproved phenomena such as poverty, prejudice, or mental illness "either are nonexistent or are even more repulsive than the actual problems themselves" (1965:385). This is what Gans (1972) concluded regarding the presence of poverty in American society: "Several of the most important functions of the poor cannot be replaced with alternatives, while some could be replaced, but almost always at higher costs to other people, particularly more affluent ones" (1972:286–287). It is unfortunately true that prejudice serves certain functions of a political or an economic nature that cannot easily be replaced. Yet such functions may affect relatively small subgroups in our society and may be irrelevant, if not dysfunctional, to numerous others.

The foregoing may have important implications for a minority group that seeks a strategy for reducing prejudice and discrimination. This can be seen most clearly perhaps in the recent history of black America. During the 1960s, significant numbers of black Americans increased their awareness of the positive functions, especially the economic functions, that prejudice and discrimination served for some groups and individuals in society. Periodicals devoted to the black protest movement emphasized the "economic exploitation of the Negro by those who occupy the top rungs of power in our contemporary exploitative society" (*Freedomways,* 1962:230). Messages communicated by certain black leaders similarly stressed the belief that economic profit for white America resulted from the continuance of large-scale forms of racism (Foner, 1970). And trends in race relations were frequently explained in terms of the *costs* to white Americans of permitting improvements for blacks relative to the *costs* of policing and servicing black ghettos (Wright, 1971).

As a reflection of a changing group consciousness, emerging black leaders stressed the importance of developing group forms of *power* and *control* as opposed to relying on the good will of the majority. Huey Newton's column in the newspaper, *The Black Panther* expressed in strong terms what was coming to be a popular point of view among black leaders and their constituents:

> The oppressor must be harassed until his doom. He must have no peace by day or by night. The slaves have always outnumbered the slavemasters. The power of the oppressor rests upon the submission of the people. When Black people really unite and rise up in all their splendid millions, they will have the strength to smash injustice. We do not understand the power in our numbers. We are millions and millions of Black people scattered across the continent and throughout the Western hemisphere. There are more Black people in America than the total population of many countries that now enjoy full membership in the United Nations. They have power and their power is based primarily on the fact that they are organized and united with each other. They are recognized by the powers of the world. [1971:426.]

It is important to inquire whether an emphasis on the power of a minority group actually represents the basis for an effective strategy for the reduction of prejudice and discrimination. The analysis in this work suggests that such an emphasis may indeed turn out to have greater effectiveness than any strategy whose major thrust relies on moral persuasion. If we are correct in our assertion that prejudice and discrimination provide gains for certain individuals and groups, then it seems unlikey that the recipients of such gains would be easily moved from their commitment to the status quo, regardless of the cogency of appeals to democracy, equalitarianism, humanism, or the like. It is more likely the case that efforts at moral persuasion would tend to be selectively perceived and distorted by those who are most anxious to protect their personality or social benefits. On the psychological level, for instance, social scientists who test the effectiveness of moral persuasion on prejudice report obtaining boomerang reactions to antiprejudice propaganda campaigns in which the persecution and victimization of minority-group members are stressed. What seems to happen is that the content of such propaganda—content that emphasizes the costs of prejudice to the *minority group*—actually *attracts* prejudiced persons who seek vicariously to satisfy their hidden desires for carrying out cruel forms of aggression on a scapegoat (Vander Zanden, 1972).

Power may provide a focus of action for minority groups that seek an active role with respect to lessening the grip of prejudice. Yet power itself can be effective only to the extent that it transcends the lines that separate majority from minority. In particular, minority-group members who themselves lack adequate resources to realize their will must be concerned with developing *coalitions,* temporary alliances in which minority-group members can participate in order to pursue a common objective.

In his discussion of black power and coalition politics,

Deutsch identifies several of the conditions under which a minority group (as a low-power group) is likely to succeed in locating allies:

> By definition, a low power group is unlikely to achieve many of its objectives unless it can find allies among significant elements within the high power group or unless it can obtain support from other ("third party") groups that can exert influence on the high power group. There is considerable reason to expect that allies are most likely to be obtained if: (1) they are sought out rather than ignored or rejected; (2) superordinate goals, common values, and common interests can be identified which could serve as a basis for the formation of cooperative bonds; (3) reasonably full communication is maintained with the potential allies; (4) one's objectives and methods are readily perceived as legitimate and feasible; (5) one's tactics dramatize one's objectives and require the potential allies to choose between acting "for" or "against" these objectives and, thus, to commit themselves to taking a position; and (6) those in high power employ tactics, as a counterresponse, which are widely viewed as "unfitting" and thus produce considerable sympathy for the low power group. [1971: 226.]

Rustin (1971) notes a tendency among spokesmen for black power to accept the historical myth that immigrant groups such as the Irish, the Jews, and the Italians were able to overcome adversities simply by sticking together as a group, making demands, and finally winning enough power to succeed. According to Rustin, the relative success of such groups depended upon their ability to form alliances with other groups (as a part of political machines or of the trade union movement) and *not* their ability singlehandedly to pull themselves up by their own bootstraps.

Blacks have similarly gained from alliances with white

groups. This has occurred either when the members of both groups have held interests in common or when whites have been aware that blacks could reciprocate favors or withhold detrimental actions against them. Glenn may well be correct when he suggests that the strongest forces continuing to operate in support of black America are "self-interested actions of powerful whites that for one reason or another benefit the Negro cause" (1965:114). It remains to be seen, however, whether the strength of such forces will be capable of overcoming the resistance imposed by those in our society who continue to benefit from the persistence of prejudice and discrimination.

SUMMARY AND CONCLUSION

We have sought to move toward an explanation for the maintenance of prejudice in our society. Prejudice has been regarded both as an *independent variable,* a causal factor that has certain consequences for society and its members, and as an *intervening variable* between important sociocultural forces, on the one hand, and individual responses, on the other. The major thrust of the chapter has been to determine why prejudice is functional. And, in this regard, we have chosen to stress the operation of competitiveness and social change as sociocultural factors of particular relevance.

To characterize American society as competitive may be to understate the obvious. Competitiveness can be found in the admiration of Americans for the acquisition of wealth, in the structure of American education, and in American socialization practices.

Implicit in competitiveness is a *psychology of scarcity,* a *zero-sum orientation* whereby individuals assume that personal gains require the losses of others. This makes possible the contributions that prejudice makes to the personality of the majority-group member, especially those contributions involving the displacement of aggression and the protection of self-esteem: If, for example, a lower-class white perceives blacks as having success, then the lower-class white may see himself as failing. As a result, he experiences a sense of relative deprivation and attempts to "keep the Negro in his place."

But the zero-sum orientation lies not only in the eyes of the beholder. It is deeply ingrained in the institutions of society. The payoff for the majority group that results from prejudice is sizable. It is the protection of its privileged position in our society—a position that carries a disproportionate amount of power, status, and economic means. Regarding the minority, competitiveness also creates many of the conditions under which special opportunities and advantages for certain of its members are produced.

Like competitiveness, social change is a factor that characterizes our society and may be functionally related to the persistence of prejudice. In relatively stable, traditional societies, it is meaningful for an individual to rely upon his previous achievements as a frame of reference for self-evaluation. By contrast, standards of evaluation in a rapidly changing, highly differentiated society tend to differ from one role to another and from one time period to the next.

As a result, the members of American society have turned toward their contemporaries in the quest for new, more meaningful standards of evaluation. Rapid change has created a need for social standards of comparison whereby individuals compare their achievements against those of their friends, classmates, or fellow employees. In the process, they strive to outdo others around them so that zero-sum thinking prevails.

The relationship between social change and prejudice can be seen in another way. Toffler has coined the term *future shock* to describe the stressful and disorienting consequences of rapid change on the individual, the kind of change that has swept across the institutions of our society. At the basis of this stress may be the individual's need for structure and his intolerance of uncertainty. A rapidly shifting social environment fails to provide adequate anchors for the events in an individual's life, leaving him without a sense of security or order. One of the consequences of prejudice for both the majority as well as the minority is to reduce cognitive and emotional uncertainties.

How do we go about reducing prejudice? On the basis of the present analysis, how do we intervene in an attempt to loosen the hold of prejudice on our society and its members? At the most fundamental level, we might begin by directing our efforts toward achieving a more cooperative, less competitive culture, in which a zero-sum orientation and prejudice have less meaning for the individual's self-esteem or his life-changes.

At the level of major institutional change, we propose focusing attention upon the structure of American formal education, a highly specialized social institution whose major function has to do with the transmission of the normative order from one generation to the next. Social scientists have long recognized that the structure of American education is largely based upon the availability of social reinforcements for academic and athletic performance. Competitiveness is emphasized, while personal improvements tends to go unnoticed.

The rewards given in educational contexts can be restructured, so that competitiveness is minimized while achievement continues to be stressed. Educational psychologists are exploring a number of reward structures that may maintain achievement and have the side effect of reducing competitiveness as well.

An effective movement away from competitiveness requires major institutional and individual change. At another level, however, we might still seek to develop strategies for the reduction of prejudice, despite the persistence of competitiveness.

Regarding personality functions of prejudice, we might devise alternative means to maintain or enhance the self-esteem of an individual. For example, personal and group forms of psychotherapy may provide a springboard for individualized efforts to reduce prejudice to the extent that they can increase insight and self-acceptance on the part of the individual.

Any slowdown in the rate of social change might contribute to an abatement in the overall level of prejudice, but would have destructive consequences as well. Rather than retard the rate of change, we must seek to discover the conditions under which individuals in society can best adapt themselves to it. We must experiment with tactics to regulate the level of stimulation from our social milieu and create educational and technological innovations to aid individuals in their ability to cope with rapid change.

To this point, we have been concerned with alternatives for such personality functions as the reduction of uncertainty and the protection of self-esteem. Given the ubiquitous presence of competitiveness, it is extremely difficult to suggest viable alternatives for the social functions of prejudice. It is unfortunately true that prejudice serves certain functions of a political and economic nature that cannot easily be replaced.

The foregoing may have important implications for a minority group that seeks a strategy for reducing prejudice and discrimination. The analysis in this work suggests that an emphasis on power may turn out to have greater effectiveness than any strategy whose major thrust relies on moral persuasion. If we are correct in asserting that prejudice provides gains for certain individuals and groups, then it seems unlikely that the recipients of such gains would be easily moved from their commitment to the status quo on the basis of appeals to democracy or humanism. Yet power itself can be effective only to the extent that it transcends the lines that separate majority from minority. Minority-group members who lack adequate resources to realize their will must be concerned with developing *coalitions,* temporary alliances in which minority-group members can participate in order to pursue a common objective.

REFERENCES

Adorno, T. W., Else Frankel-Brunswick, Daniel J. Levinson, and Nevitt H. Sanford 1950 *The Authoritarian Personality*. New York: Harper & Row.

Allport, Gordon W. 1954 *The Nature of Prejudice*. Reading, Mass.: Addison-Wesley.

Armendáriz, Albert 1967 *The Mexican American: A New Focus of Opportunity*. Washington, D.C.: GPO.

Barcus, F. Earle and Jack Levin 1966 "Role Distance in Negro and Majority Fiction." *Journalism Quarterly* (Winter): 709–714.

Bellisfield, Gwen 1972–1973 "White Attitudes Toward Racial Integration and the Urban Riots of the 1960's." *Public Opinion Quarterly* (Winter): 579–584.

Berelson, Bernard and Patricia Salter 1946 "Majority and Minority Americans: An Analysis of Magazine Fiction." *Public Opinion Quarterly* (Summer): 168–190.

Berkowitz, Leonard 1962 Aggression: *A Social Psychological Analysis*. New York: McGraw-Hill.

Berry, Brewton 1965 *Race and Ethnic Relations*. Boston: Houghton Mifflin.

Bettelheim, Bruno and Morris Janowitz 1964 *Social Change and Prejudice*. New York: Free Press.

Blalock, Hubert M., Jr. 1967 *Toward a Theory of Minority-Group Relations*. New York: Wiley.

Blassingame, John W. 1972 *The Slave Community*. New York: Oxford University Press.

Blauner, Robert 1972 *Racial Oppression in America*. New York: Harper & Row.

Block, J. and Jeanne Block 1951 "An Investigation of the Relationship Between Intolerance of Ambiguity and Ethnocentrism." *Journal of Personality* 19: 303–311.

Bogardus, Emory S. 1925 "Measuring Social Distance." *Journal of Applied Sociology* (March–April): 299–308.

Bonacich, Edna 1972 "A Theory of Ethnic Antagonism: The Split Labor Market." *American Sociological Review* (October): 547–559.

Brigham, Carl C. 1923 *A Study of American Intelligence*. Princeton, N.J.: Princeton University Press.

Brigham, John and Theodore Weissbach 1972 *Racial Attitudes in America*. New York: Harper & Row.

Brink, William and Louis Harris 1964 *The Negro Revolution in America*. New York: Simon & Schuster.

Brink, William and Louis Harris 1967 *Black and White*. New York: Simon & Schuster.

Brody, Jane E. 1973 "Doctors Study Treatment of Ills Brought on by Stress." *The New York Times* (June 10): 20.

Burke, Peter J. 1969 "Scapegoating: An Alternative to Role Differentiation." *Sociometry* (June): 159–168.

Burkey, Richard M. 1971 *Racial Discrimination and Public Policy in the United States*. Lexington, Mass.: Heath.

Burnette, Robert 1971 *The Tortured Americans*. Englewood Cliffs, N.J.: Prentice-Hall.

Burnstein, Eugene and Philip Worchel 1962 "Arbitrariness of Frustration and Its Consequences for Aggression in a Social Situation." *Journal of Personality* 30: 528–541.

Campbell, Angus 1971 *White Attitudes Toward Black People*. Ann Arbor, Mich.: University of Michigan Press.

Carmichael, Stokely and Charles V. Hamilton 1967 *Black Power*. New York: Random House.

Caudill, William and George de Vos 1966 "Achievement, Culture, and Personality." Pp. 77–89 in Bernard E. Segal, *Racial and Ethnic Relations.* New York: T. Y. Crowell.

Chinoy, Ely 1961 *Society*. New York: Random House.

Chorover, Stephan L. 1973 "Big Brother and Psychotechnology." *Psychology Today* (October): 43–54.

Christie, Richard, Joan Havel, and Bernard Seidenberg 1958 "Is the F Scale Irreversible?" *Journal of Abnormal and Social Psychology* (March): 143–159.

Clark, Kenneth B. and Mamie P. Clark 1958 "Racial Identification and Preference in Negro Children." Pp. 169–178 in Eleanor E. Maccoby, Theodore M. Newcomb, and Eugene L. Hartley (eds.), *Readings in Social Psychology*. New York: Holt, Rinehart & Winston.

Cloward, Richard A. and Lloyd E. Ohlin 1960 *Delinquency and Opportunity*. New York Free Press.

Cole, Stewart G. and Mildred Wiese 1954 *Minorities and the American Promise*. New York: Harper & Row.

Coleman, James S. 1963 "Academic Achievement and the Structure of Competition." Pp. 212–229 in Neil J. Smelser and William T. Smelser (eds.). *Personality and Social Systems*. New York: Wiley.

Colfax, J. David and Susan Frankel Sternberg 1972 "The Perpetuation of Racial Stereotypes: Blacks in Mass Circulation Magazine Advertisements." *Public Opinion Quarterly* (Spring): 8–17.

Comer, James P. 1972 *Beyond Black and White*. Chicago: Quadrangle.

Commission on the Cities in the '70's 1972 *Report*. New York: Praeger.

Constantini, Arthur F., Jack Davis, John R. Braun, and Annette Iervolino 1973 "Personality and Mood Correlates of Schedule of Recent Experience Scores." *Psychological Reports* 32: 1143–1150.

Cook, Thomas J. 1970 "Benign Neglect: Minimum Feasible Understanding." *Social Problems* (Fall): 145–152.

Coser, Lewis A. 1956 *The Functions of Social Conflict*. New York: Free Press.

Coser, Lewis A. 1972 "The Alien as a Servant of Power: Court Jews and Christian Renegades." *American Sociological Review* (October): 574–581.

Couch, Arthur and Kenneth Keniston 1960 "Yeasayers and Naysayers: Agreeing Response Set as a Personality Variable." *Journal of Abnormal and Social Psychology* (March): 151–174.

Cowen, Emory L., Judith Landes, and Donald E. Schaet 1959 "The Effects of Mild Frustration on the Expression of Prejudiced Attitudes." *Journal of Abnormal and Social Psychology* (January): 33–38.

DeFleur, Melvin L., William V. D'Antonio, and Lois B. DeFleur 1971 *Sociology: Man in Society*. Glenview, Ill.: Scott, Foresman.

Deloria, Vine Jr. 1970 *We Talk, You Listen*. New York: Delta.

Derbyshire, Robert L., and Eugene Brody 1964 "Social Distance and Identity Conflict in Negro College Students." *Sociology and Social Research* (April): 301–314.

Deutsch, Morton 1953 "The Effects of Cooperation and Competition upon Group Process." Pp. 319–353 in D. Cartwright and A. Zander (eds.), *Group Dynamics*. New York: Harper & Row.

Deutsch, Morton 1971 "Strategies for Powerless Groups." Pp. 223–228 in Gary T. Marx (ed.), *Racial Conflict*. Boston: Little, Brown.

Dimont, Max I. 1962 *Jews, God and History*. New York: Signet.

Dollard, John   1937   *Caste and Class in a Southern Town*. New Haven, Conn.: Yale University Press.

Dollard, John   1938   "Hostility and Fear in Social Life." *Social Forces* (October): 15–26.

Dollard, John, Leonard W. Doob, Neal E. Miller, O. H. Mowrer, and Robert R. Sears   1939   *Frustration and Aggression*. New Haven, Conn.: Yale University Press.

Douglas, Jack D.   1970   *Deviance and Respectability*. New York: Basic Books.

Dunbar, Paul Laurence   1940   *The Complete Poems of Paul Laurence Dunbar*. New York: Dodd, Mead.

Durkheim, Emile   1933   *The Division of Labor in Society*. New York: Macmillan.

Edwards, Richard C., Michael Reich, and Thomas E. Weisskopf (eds.)   1972   *The Capitalist System*. Englewood Cliffs, N.J.: Prentice-Hall.

Ehrlich, Howard J.   1973   *The Social Psychology of Prejudice*. New York: Wiley.

Eitzen, D. Stanley   1970   "Status Inconsistency and Wallace Supporters in a Midwestern City." *Social Forces* (June): 493–498.

El Gallo   1968   "La Raza Quiz." (March): 23.

Faris, R. E. L. (ed.)   1964   *Handbook of Modern Sociology*. Skokie, Ill.: Rand McNally.

Flax, Michael J.   1971   *Blacks and Whites: An Experiment in Racial Indicators*. Washington, D.C.: The Urban Institute.

Foner, Philip S. (ed.)   1970   *The Black Panthers Speak*. Philadelphia: Lippincott.

Franklin, John Hope and Isidore Starr (eds.)   1967   *The Negro in 20th Century America*. New York: Vintage.

Frazier, E. Franklin   1951   "The Negro's Vested Interest in Segregation." Pp. 332–339 in Arnold M. Rose (ed.), *Race Prejudice and Discrimination*. New York: Knopf.

Freedomways   1962   "The Economic Status of Negroes." (Summer): 230.

Gallagher, James J.   1970   *Teaching the Gifted Child*. Boston: Allyn & Bacon.

Gans, Herbert J.   1972   "The Positive Functions of Poverty." *American Journal of Sociology* (September): 275–289.

Geen, Russell G.   1972   *Aggression*. Morristown, New Jersey: General Learning Press.

Genovese, Eugene D.   1969   *The World the Slaveholders Made*. New York: Pantheon.

Gerth, H. H. and C. W. Mills (eds.)   1946   *From Max Weber: Essays in Sociology*. New York: Oxford University Press.

Gilbert, G. M.   1951   "Stereotype Persistence and Change Among College Students." *Journal of Abnormal and Social Psychology* (April): 245–254.

Glenn, Norval D. 1963 "Occupational Benefits to Whites from the Subordination of Negroes." *American Sociological Review* (June): 443–448.

Glenn, Norval D. 1965 "The Role of White Resistance and Facilitation in the Negro Struggle for Equality." *Phylon* (Summer): 105–116.

Glenn, Norval D. 1966 "White Gains from Negro Subordination." *Social Problems* (Fall): 159–178.

Golden, Harry 1962 *you're entitle'*. New York: Crest.

Golden, Patricia M. 1974 "Status-Concern, Authoritarianism, and Prejudice." Mimeo paper, Northeastern University.

Gordon, Milton M. 1964 *Assimilation in American Life*. New York: Oxford University Press.

Gorer, Geoffrey 1964 *The American People*. New York: Norton.

Greenwald, Herbert J. 1973 "Implications for Change Derived From a Theory of Hierarchical Dispositions," Mimeo paper.

Greenwald, Herbert J. and Don B. Oppenheim 1968 "Reported Magnitude of Self-Misidentification Among Negro Children—an Artifact?" *Journal of Personality and Social Psychology* (January): 49–52.

Haimowitz, Morris L. and Natalie R. Haimowitz 1950 "Reducing Ethnic Hostility Through Psychotherapy." *Journal of Social Psychology* (May): 231–241.

Hakmiller, Karl L. 1966 "Threat as a Determinant of Downward Comparison." *Journal of Experimental Social Psychology* Supplement 1 (September): 32–39.

Handlin, Oscar 1962 *The Newcomers*. Garden City, N.Y.: Anchor.

Harris, Marvin 1964 *Patterns of Race in the Americas*. New York: Walker.

Heer, David M. 1959 "The Sentiment of White Supremacy: An Ecological Study." *American Journal of Sociology* (May): 592–598.

Heiss, Jerold and Susan Owens 1972 "Self-Evaluations of Blacks and Whites." *American Journal of Sociology* (September): 360–370.

Henry, A. F. and J. F. Short, Jr. 1954 *Suicide and Homicide*. New York: Free Press.

Henry, Jules 1969 "American Schoolrooms: Learning the Nightmare." Pp. 202–209 in Richard C. Sprinthall and Norman A. Sprinthall (eds.), *Educational Psychology*. New York: Van Nostrand Reinhold.

Herrnstein, Richard J. 1971 "I.Q." *The Atlantic* (September): 43–64.

Hofman, John E. 1970 "The Meaning of Being a Jew in Israel: An Analysis of Ethnic Identity." *Journal of Personality and Social Psychology* (July): 196–202.

Holmes, David S. 1972 "Aggression, Displacement, and Guilt." *Journal of Personality and Social Psychology* (March): 296–301.

Holmes, Thomas H. and Richard H. Rahe 1967 "The Social Readjustment Rating Scale." *Journal of Psychosomatic Research* 11: 213–218.

Horney, Karen 1937 *The Neurotic Personality of Our Time*. New York: Norton.

Hovland, Carl I. and Robert R. Sears 1940 "Minor Studies of Aggression: Correlation of Lynchings with Economic Indices." *Journal of Psychology* (Winter): 301–310.

Howard, David H. 1966 "An Exploratory Study of Attitudes of Negro Professionals Toward Competition with Whites." *Social Forces* (Summer): 20–27.

Howe, Florence and Paul Lauter 1972 "How the School System Is Rigged for Failure." Pp. 229–235 in Richard C. Edwards, Michael Reich, and Thomas E. Weisskopf (eds.), *The Capitalist System*. Englewood Cliffs, N.J.: Prentice-Hall.

Hughes, Langston 1968 "Tales of Simple." Pp. 97–112 in Abraham Chapman (ed.), *Black Voices*. New York: Mentor.

Hyman, Herbert H. and Paul B. Sheatsley 1956 "Attitudes Toward Desegregation." *Scientific American* 195: 35–39.

Hyman, Herbert H. and Paul B. Sheatsley 1964 "Attitudes Toward Desegregation." *Scientific American* 211: 16–23.

Hyman, Herbert H. and Eleanor Singer (eds.) 1968 *Readings in Reference Group Theory and Research*. New York: Free Press.

Jacobs, Paul and Saul Landau with Eve Pell 1971 *To Serve the Devil*. Vol. I. New York: Vintage.

Jenson, Arthur R. 1969 "How Much Can We Boost IQ and Scholastic Achievement?" Pp. 1–123 in *Environment, Heredity, and Intelligence*. Harvard Educational Review Reprint Series No. 2. Cambridge, Mass.: Harvard University Press.

Kagan, S. and M. C. Madsen 1972 "Experimental Analyses of Cooperation and Competition of Anglo-American and Mexican Children." *Developmental Psychology* 6: 49–59.

Kamin, Leon 1973 "War of IQ: Indecisive Genes." *Intellectual Digest* (December): 22–23.

Karlins, Marvin, Thomas L. Coffman, and Gary Walters 1969 "On the Fading of Social Stereotypes: Studies in Three Generations of College Students." *Journal of Personality and Social Psychology* (September): 1–16.

Katz, Daniel 1960 "The Functional Approach to the Study of Attitudes." *Public Opinion Quarterly* (Summer): 163–204.

Katz, David and Kenneth Braly 1933 "Racial Stereotypes of One Hundred College Students." *Journal of Abnormal and Social Psychology* (October-December): 280–290.

Kaufman, Walter 1957 "Status, Authoritarianism, and Anti-Semitism." *American Journal of Sociology* (January): 379–382.

Killian, Lewis M. 1968 *The Impossible Revolution*. New York: Random House.

King, Larry L. 1969 *Confessions of a White Racist*. New York: Viking.

Knapp, Melvin J. and Jon P. Alston 1972–1973 "White Parental Acceptance of Varying Degrees of School Desegregation: 1965 and 1970." *Public Opinion Quarterly* (Winter): 585–591.

Koenig, Fredrick W. and Morton B. King, Jr. 1962 "Cognitive Simplicity and Prejudice." *Social Forces* (March): 220–222.

Kramer, Bernard M. 1949 "Dimensions of Prejudice," *The Journal of Psychology* 27: 389–451.

La Gumina, Salvatore J. 1973 *Wop!* San Francisco: Straight Arrow.

Lam, Margaret M. 1936 "Racial Myth and Family Tradition-Worship Among Part-Hawaiians." *Social Forces* (March): 149–157.

Lazarwitz, Bernard 1970 "Contrasting the Effects of Generation, Class, Sex, and Age on Group Identification in the Jewish and Protestant Communities." *Social Forces* (September): 50–59.

Leibowitz, Lila 1973 "Perspectives on the Evolution of Sex Differences." Paper presented at the American Anthropological Association Meetings.

Lerner, Janet W. 1971 *Children with Learning Disabilities*. Boston: Houghton Mifflin.

Lerner, Max 1957 *America as a Civilization*. Vol. II. New York: Simon & Schuster.

Lerner, Max 1972 "People and Places." Pp. 103–119 in Peter I. Rose (ed.), *Nation of Nations*. New York: Random House.

Levin, Jack 1969 "The Influence of Social Comparison on Displaced Aggression." Paper presented at the Eastern Psychological Association Meetings.

Levin, Jack and William J. Leong 1973 "Comparative Reference Group Behavior and Assimilation." *Phylon* (September): 289–294.

Levin, Jack and James L. Spates 1970 "Hippie Values: An Analysis of the Underground Press." *Youth and Society* (September): 59–73.

Levin, William C. and Jack Levin 1973 "Social Comparison of Grades: The Influence of Mode of Comparison and Machiavellianism." *Journal of Social Psychology* 91: 67–72.

Levy, Sheldon G. 1972 "Polarization in Racial Attitudes." *Public Opinion Quarterly* (Summer): 221–234.

Lewis, Oscar 1968 "The Culture of Poverty." Pp. 187–200 in Daniel P. Moynihan (ed.), *On Understanding Poverty*. New York: Basic Books.

Lippitt, Ronald and Ralph K. White 1958 "An Experimental Study of Leadership and Group Life." Pp. 496–510 in Eleanor E. Maccoby,

Theodore M. Newcomb, and Eugene L. Hartley (eds.), *Readings in Social Psychology*. New York: Holt, Rinehart & Winston.

Lippmann, Walter 1922 *Public Opinion*. New York: Harcourt Brace Jovanovich.

Littleton, Arthur C. and Mary W. Burger 1971 *Black Viewpoints*. New York: Mentor.

Logan, Rayford W. 1954 *The Betrayal of the Negro*. New York: Collier.

London, Joan and Henry Anderson 1970 *So Shall Ye Reap*. New York: T. Y. Crowell.

Lynch, Helen 1972 "Equality Would Be a Demotion." *Sunday Herald Traveler* (*Pictorial Living*) (October 15): 4.

McCarthy, John D. and William L. Yancey 1971 "Uncle Tom and Mr. Charlie: Metaphysical Pathos in the Study of Racism and Personal Disorganization." *American Journal of Sociology* (January): 648–672.

Maccoby, Eleanor, Theodore M. Newcomb, and Eugene L. Hartley 1958 *Readings in Social Psychology*. New York: Holt, Rinehart & Winston.

MacDonald, Kenneth W. 1971 "The Relationship of Classical Predictors of Prejudice to Attitudes Toward Black Power." Unpublished M.A. thesis, Kent State University.

Mangum, Paul L. 1973 "Role Change, Intolerance of Ambiguity, and Psychological Stress." Unpublished M.A. thesis, Northeastern University.

McManus, J. T., and Louis Kronenberger 1946 "Motion Pictures, the Theater, and Race Relations." *Annals of the American Academy of Political and Social Science* (March): 152–157.

McWilliams, Carey 1948 *A Mask for Privilege: Anti-Semitism in America*. Boston: Little, Brown.

Martin, James and Frank Westie 1959 "The Tolerant Personality." *American Sociological Review* 24: 524–531.

Martínez, Thomas M. 1969 "Advertising and Racism: The Case of the Mexican-American." El Grito (Summer): 2.

Marx, Gary T. (ed.) 1971 *Racial Conflict*. Boston: Little, Brown.

Megargee, Edwin I. and Jack E. Hokanson (eds.) 1970 *The Dynamics of Aggression* New York: Harper & Row.

Meier, August and Elliot M. Rudwick 1966 *From Plantation to Ghetto*. New York: Hill & Wang.

Merton, Robert K. 1957 *Social Theory and Social Structure*. New York: Free Press.

Metzger, Paul L. 1971 "American Sociology and Black Assimilation: Conflicting Perspectives." *American Journal of Sociology* (January): 627–647.

Miller, L. Keith and Robert L. Hamblin 1963 "Interdependence, Differential Rewarding and Productivity." *American Sociological Review* 28: 768–778.

Miller, Neal E. and Richard Bugelski 1948 "Minor Studies of Aggression: The Influence of Frustrations Imposed by the In-Group on Attitudes Expressed Toward Out-groups." *Journal of Psychology* 25: 437–442.

Minturn, L. and W. W. Lambert 1964 *Mothers of Six Cultures—Antecedents of Child Rearing.* New York: Wiley.

Morland, J. Kenneth 1969 "Race Awareness Among American and Hong Kong Chinese Children." *American Journal of Sociology* (November): 360–374.

Morland, J. Kenneth 1972 "Racial Acceptance and Preference of Nursery School Children in a Southern City." Pp. 51–58 in John Brigham and Theodore Weissbach (eds.), *Racial Attitudes in America.* New York: Harper & Row.

Moynihan, Daniel P. 1965 The Negro Family: *The Case for National Action.* United States Department of Labor. Washington, D.C.: GPO.

Moynihan, Daniel P. (ed.) 1968 *On Understanding Poverty.* New York: Basic Books.

Myrdal, Gunnar (with the assistance of Richard Sterner and Arnold Rose) 1944 *An American Dilemma.* New York: Harper & Row.

Neill, A. S. 1960 *Summerhill: A Radical Approach to Child Rearing.* New York: Hart.

Nelson, Linden L. and Spencer Kagan 1972 "Competition: The Star-Spangled Scramble." *Psychology Today* (September): 53–56, 90–91.

Newton, Huey P. 1971 "In Defense of Self-Defense." Pp. 424–427 in Arthur C. Littleton and Mary W. Burger (eds.), *Black Viewpoints.* New York: Mentor.

Noel, Donald L. 1968 "A Theory of the Origin of Ethnic Stratification." *Social Problems* (Fall): 157–172.

O'Hara, Robert C. 1961 *Media for the Millions.* New York: Random House.

Palmer, Stuart 1960 *The Psychology of Murder.* New York: T. Y. Crowell.

Parker, Seymour and Robert J. Kleiner 1968 "Reference Group Behavior and Mental Disorder." Pp. 350–373 in Herbert H. Hyman and Eleanor Singer (eds.), *Readings in Reference Group Theory and Research.* New York: Free Press.

Parsons, Talcott and Kenneth B. Clark (eds.) 1966 *The Negro American.* Boston: Houghton Mifflin.

Petroni, Frank A. 1972 "Adolescent Liberalism—The Myth of a Generation Gap." *Adolescence* (Summer): 221–232.

Pettigrew, Thomas F. 1964 *A Profile of the Negro American.* New

York: Van Nostrand Reinhold.

Pettigrew, Thomas F. 1971 *Racially Separate or Together?* New York: McGraw-Hill.

Pettigrew, Thomas F., Robert T. Riley, and Reeve D. Vanneman 1972 "George Wallace's Constituents." *Psychology Today* (February): 47–49, 92.

Phillips, Bernard S. 1969 Sociology: *Social Structure and Change.* New York: Macmillan.

Prosterman, Roy L. 1972 *Surviving to 3000.* Belmont, California: Duxbury Press.

Rainwater, Lee 1966 "Crucible of Identity: The Negro Lower-Case Family." Pp. 167–181 in Talcott Parsons and Kenneth B. Clark (eds.), *The Negro American.* Boston: Houghton Mifflin.

Redding, Saunders 1950 *They Came in Chains.* Philadelphia: Lippincott.

Reich, Charles A. 1970 *The Greening of America.* New York: Random House.

Reich, Michael 1972 "The Economics of Racism." Pp. 313–321 in Richard C. Edwards, Michael Reich, and Thomas E. Weisskopf (eds.), *The Capitalist System.* Englewood Cliffs, N.J.: Prentice-Hall.

Rogers, Carl R. 1969 "The Facilitation of Significant Learning." Pp. 172–182 in Richard C. Sprinthall and Norman A. Sprinthall (eds.), *Educational Psychology.* New York: Van Nostrand Reinhold.

Rokeach, Milton 1952 "Attitude as a Determinant of Recall." *Journal of Abnormal and Social Psychology* 47: 482–488.

Rokeach, Milton 1960 *The Open and Closed Mind.* New York: Basic Books.

Rose, Arnold M. (ed.) 1951 *Race Prejudice and Discrimination.* New York: Knopf.

Rose, Arnold M. 1958 *The Roots of Prejudice.* New York: United Nations, UNESCO.

Rose, Peter I. (ed.) 1972 Nation of Nations: *The Ethnic Experience and the Racial Crisis.* New York: Random House.

Rose, Peter I. 1974 *They and We.* New York: Random House.

Rosnow, Ralph L. 1972 "Poultry and Prejudice." *Psychology Today* (March): 53–56.

Rosnow, Ralph L., Robert F. Holz, and Jack Levin 1966 "Differential Effects of Complementary and Competing Variables in Primacy-Recency." *Journal of Social Psychology* 69: 135–147.

Rossi, Peter H. 1972 "Alienation in the White Community." Pp. 289–293 in Peter I. Rose (ed.), *Nation of Nations: The Ethnic Experience and the Racial Crisis.* New York: Random House.

Rubin, Irwin M. 1967 "Increased Self-Acceptance: A Means of Reducing Prejudice." *Journal of Personality and Social Psychology* 5: 233–238.

Rule, Brendan G. and Elizabeth Percival 1971 "The Effects of Frustration and Attack on Physical Aggression." *Journal of Experimental Research on Personality* 5: 111–188.

Rustin, Bayard 1971 "'Black Power' and Coalition Politics." Pp. 193–200 in Gary T. Marx, *Racial Conflict*. Boston: Little, Brown.

Ryan, William 1971 *Blaming the Victim*. New York: Vintage.

Sagarin, Edward (ed.) 1971 *The Other Minorities*. Boston: Ginn.

Sartre, Jean-Paul 1965 *Anti-Semite and Jew*. New York: Schocken.

Scodel, Alvin and Paul Mussen 1953 "Social Perceptions of Authoritarians and Nonauthoritarians." *Journal of Abnormal and Social Psychology*, 48: pp. 181–184.

Segal, Bernard E. (ed.) 1966 *Racial and Ethnic Relations*. New York: T. Y. Crowell.

Selznick, Gertrude J. and Stephen Steinberg 1969 *The Tenacity of Prejudice*. New York: Harper & Row.

Sherif, Muzafer, et al. 1961 *Intergroup Conflict and Cooperation: The Robbers Cave Experiment*. Norman: Institute of Intergroup Relations, University of Oklahoma.

Sherif, Muzafer and Carolyn W. Sherif 1956 *An Outline of Social Psychology*. New York: Harper & Row.

Sherman, Howard 1972 *Radical Political Economy*. New York: Basic Books.

Shuey, Audrey M. 1953 "Stereotyping of Negroes and Whites: An Analysis of Magazine Pictures." *Public Opinion Quarterly* 17: 281–292.

Silberman, Charles E. 1964 *Crisis in Black and White*. New York: Random House.

Simmel, Georg 1955 *Conflict*. New York: Free Press.

Simmen, Edward (ed.) 1972 *Pain and Promise: The Chicano Today*. New York: Mentor.

Simmons, Ozzie G. 1961 "The Mutual Images and Expectations of Anglo-Americans and Mexican-Americans." *Daedalus* (Spring): 286–299.

Simpson, George E. and J. Milton Yinger 1972 *Racial and Cultural Minorities: An Analysis of Prejudice and Discrimination*. New York: Harper & Row.

Sinha, Gopal Sharan and Ramesh Chandra Sinha 1967 "Explorations in Caste Stereotypes." *Social Forces* (September): 42–47.

Smelser, Neil J. and William T. Smelser (eds.) 1963 *Personality and Social Systems*. New York: Wiley.

Smythe, Dallas W. 1954 "Reality as Presented by Television." *Public Opinion Quarterly* 18: 143–156.

Sorkin, Alan L. 1969 "Education, Migration and Negro Unemployment." *Social Forces* (March): 265–274.

Spiegalman, M., C. Terwilliger, and F. Fearing 1953 "The Content

of Comics: Goals and Means to Goals of Comic Strip Characters."
Journal of Social Psychology 37: 189–203.

Sprinthall, Richard C. and Norman A. Sprinthall (eds.) 1969 *Educational Psychology*. New York: Van Nostrand Reinhold.

Srole, Leo 1956 "Social Integration and Certain Corollaries: An Exploratory Study." *American Sociological Review* (December): 709–716.

Stagner, R. and C. S. Congdon 1955 "Another Failure to Demonstrate Displacement of Aggression." *Journal of Abnormal and Social Psychology* 51: 696–697.

Stampp, Kenneth M. 1956 *The Peculiar Institution*. New York: Vintage.

Steiner, Ivan D. and Homer H. Johnson 1963 "Authoritarianism and Conformity." *Sociometry* (March): 21–34.

Stember, Charles Herbert 1961 *Education and Attitude Change: The Effect of Schooling on Prejudice Against Minority Groups*. Institute of Human Relations.

Strauss, Helen May 1968 "Reference Group and Social Comparison Processes Among the Totally Blind." Pp. 222–237 in Herbert H. Hyman and Eleanor Singer (eds.), *Readings in Reference Group Theory and Research*. New York: Free Press.

Sung, B. L. 1961 *The Mountain of Gold: The Story of the Chinese in America*. New York: Macmillan.

Sweeny, Arthur 1922 "Mental Tests for Immigrants." *North American Review* (May): 600–612. TenHouten, Warren D. et al. 1971 "School Ethnic Composition, Social Contexts, and Educational Plans of Mexican-American and Anglo High School Students. *American Journal of Sociology* (July): 89–107.

Toffler, Alvin 1970 *Future Shock*. New York: Bantam.

Torrence, W. and Paul Meadows 1958 "American Culture Themes." *Sociology and Social Research* 43: 3–7.

Triandis, Harry C. and Leigh M. Triandis 1972 "Some Studies of Social Distance." Pp. 97–105 in John Brigham and Theodore Weissbach (eds.), *Racial Attitudes in America*. New York: Harper & Row.

Tumin, Melvin 1965 "The Functionalist Approach to Social Problems." *Social Problems* (Spring): 379–388.

Turner, Ralph H. 1960 "Preoccupation with Competitiveness and Social Acceptance among American and English College Students." *Sociometry* 23: 307–325.

U.S. Advisory Commission on Civil Disorders 1968 *Report*. New York: Bantam.

van den Berghe, Pierre L. 1966 "Paternalistic Versus Competitive Race Relations: An Ideal-Type Approach." Pp. 53–69 in Bernard E. Segal (ed.), *Racial and Ethnic Relations*. New York: T. Y. Crowell.

van den Haag, Ernest 1969 *The Jewish Mystique*. New York: Dell.

Vander Zanden, James W.   1960   "The Klan Revival." *American Journal of Sociology* (March): 456–462.

Vander Zanden, James W.   1972   *American Minority Relations.* New York: Ronald.

Wahrhaftig, Albert L. and Robert K. Thomas   1969   "Renaissance and Repression: The Oklahoma Cherokee." *Transaction* (February): 42–48.

Westie, Frank R.   1964   "Race and Ethnic Relations." Pp. 576–618 in R. E. L. Faris (ed.), *Handbook of Modern Sociology.* Skokie, Ill.: Rand McNally.

White, Ralph K. and Ronald Lippitt   1960   *Autocracy and Democracy: An Experimental Inquiry.* New York: Harper & Row.

Wilhelm, Sidney M.   1970   *Who Needs the Negro?* Cambridge, Mass.: Schenkman.

Williams, Robin M., Jr.   1947   *The Reduction of Intergroup Tensions.* Bulletin No. 57. New York: Social Science Research Council.

Williams, Robin M., Jr.   1964   *Strangers Next Door.* Englewood Cliffs, N.J.: Prentice-Hall.

Williams, Robin M., Jr.   1965   *American Society.* New York: Knopf.

Wilson, Stephen R. and Larry A. Benner   1971   "The Effects of Self-Esteem and Situation upon Comparison Choices During Ability Evaluation." *Sociometry* (September): 381–397.

Woodward, C. Vann   1955   *The Strange Career of Jim Crow.* New York: Oxford University Press.

Wright, Nathan Jr.   1971   "The Economics of Race." Pp. 305–313 in Arthur C. Littleton and Mary W. Burger (eds.), *Black Viewpoints.* New York: Mentor.

Yancey, William L., Leo Rigsby, and John D. McCarthy   1972   "Social Position and Self-Evaluation: The Relative Importance of Race." *American Journal of Sociology* (September): 338–359.

Yinger, J. Milton   1961   "Social Forces Involved in Group Identification or Withdrawal." *Daedalus* (Spring): 247–262.

INDEX